Stress-Free
Weaning
Judy More

For UK order enquiries: please contact Bookpoint Ltd, 130 Milton Park, Abingdon, Oxon OX14 4SB. Telephone: +44 (0) 1235 827720. Fax: +44 (0) 1235 400454. Lines are open 09.00–17.00, Monday to Saturday, with a 24-hour message answering service. Details about our titles and how to order are available at www.teachyourself.co.uk

For USA order enquiries: please contact McGraw-Hill Customer Services, PO Box 545, Blacklick, OH 43004-0545, USA. Telephone: 1-800-722-4726. Fax: 1-614-755-5645.

For Canada order enquiries: please contact McGraw-Hill Ryerson Ltd, 300 Water St, Whitby, Ontario L1N 9B6, Canada. Telephone: 905 430 5000. Fax: 905 430 5020.

Long renowned as the authoritative source for self-guided learning – with more than 50 million copies sold worldwide – the **Teach Yourself** series includes over 500 titles in the fields of languages, crafts, hobbies, business, computing and education.

British Library Cataloguing in Publication Data: a catalogue record for this title is available from the British Library.

Library of Congress Catalog Card Number: on file.

First published in UK 2007 by Hodder Education, part of Hachette UK, 338 Euston Road, London, NW1 3BH.

First published in US 2007 by The McGraw-Hill Companies, Inc.

This edition published 2010.

Previously published as *Teach Yourself Feeding Your Baby.*

The **Teach Yourself** name is a registered trade mark of Hodder Headline.

Typeset by MPS Limited, a Macmillan Company.

Printed in Great Britain for Hodder Education, an Hachette UK Company, 338 Euston Road, London NW1 3BH, by CPI Cox & Wyman, Reading, Berkshire RG1 8EX.

The publisher has used its best endeavours to ensure that the URLs for external websites referred to in this book are correct and active at the time of going to press. However, the publisher and the author have no responsibility for the websites and can make no guarantee that a site will remain live or that the content will remain relevant, decent or appropriate.

Hachette UK's policy is to use papers that are natural, renewable and recyclable products and made from wood grown in sustainable forests. The logging and manufacturing processes are expected to conform to the environmental regulations of the country of origin.

Impression number   10 9 8 7 6 5 4 3 2

Year   2014 2013 2012 2011 2010

Acknowledgements

Throughout my career I have worked with many parents, children and healthcare professionals who have influenced my understanding of childhood nutrition and how best to feed babies. Those whose work and collaboration has particularly influenced the content of this book are Dr Gillian Harris, Dr Carina Venter, Dr Helen Crawley and Professor Lawrence Weaver.

Image credits

Front cover: © Dorling Kindersley/Getty Images

Back cover: © Jakub Semeniuk/iStockphoto.com, © Royalty-Free/Corbis, © agencyby/iStockphoto.com, © Andy Cook/iStockphoto.com, © Christopher Ewing/iStockphoto.com, © zebicho – Fotolia.com, © Geoffrey Holman/iStockphoto.com, © Photodisc/Getty Images, © James C. Pruitt/iStockphoto.com, © Mohamed Saber – Fotolia.com

Contents

Meet the author

I have loved being a nutritionist and dietician ever since
I graduated from university having studied nutrition and
dietetics. Food quality, food choices and the health implications
of what we choose to eat is a fascinating subject. I specialized in
children about 20 years ago and worked as a paediatric dietician
in teaching hospitals and in the community. Learning through
working with psychologists, speech and language therapists,
health visitors, doctors and midwives in multidisciplinary clinics
has given me a wider view on feeding than just nutrition. Advice
on feeding babies needs to take account of psychology, the way
babies develop and parents' attitudes to food in addition to the
nutritional needs of the baby. Feeding my own two children and
their friends and talking to hundreds of parents about feeding
their children has given me an inside view on how different each
child and family can be. I set up the Child-nutrition consultancy
(www.child-nutrition.co.uk) about ten years ago to provide the
best advice on feeding babies and deal with today's challenges
of poor diets and rising UK rates of rickets and obesity. I keep
abreast of the latest research on feeding babies and children;
advise food companies, nurseries, schools and government
agencies; teach students; train healthcare professionals and write
about feeding babies and children in addition to seeing babies
and children with their parents in a weekly clinic.

Judy More

Only got a minute?

Your baby only needs breast milk or infant formula milk up until four to six months of age. Breast milk is preferable because it protects against illness. Babies should start to be weaned onto solid food by six months. They all develop at different rates, and some will be ready sooner, but no weaning should begin before four months. Breastfeeding while weaning reduces the risk of some diseases.

Weaning starts with smooth purées, progresses onto mashed foods with soft lumps and soft finger foods by around six to seven months, and finally onto minced and chopped foods with hard finger foods. Along the way babies also learn to sip from a cup or beaker, self-feed with finger foods and begin using a spoon. By 12 months babies should be eating the same foods as the rest of the family, although some foods may still need to be cut into smaller pieces for them. After 12 months bottles of milk should be discontinued and milk reduced to being part of a balanced diet that includes foods from all five food groups.

5 Only got five minutes?

Your baby only needs breast milk or formula milk up until four to six months of age. Breast milk is preferable because it protects against illness which formula milk does not. Babies should start to be weaned onto solid food by six months. They all develop at different rates, and while some can wait until just before six months others will be ready sooner. No weaning should begin before four months, and if a mother is still breastfeeding during weaning onto solid foods, the risk of childhood diabetes and some food allergies is reduced.

Weaning is a gradual process, starting with smooth purées, progressing to mashed foods with soft lumps and soft finger foods by six to seven months, and finally onto minced and chopped foods with hard finger foods from about nine months. Along the way babies also learn to sip from a cup or beaker, self-feed with finger foods and begin using a spoon.

Weaning is a learning process and babies only learn to eat new tastes and textures by having the opportunity to learn to like them. Offering new foods and textures frequently gives them this opportunity. By 12 months babies should be eating the same foods as the rest of the family, although some foods may still need to be cut into smaller pieces for them.

During your baby's second year he is likely to become more fussy about which foods he will eat. This is a natural stage of development, protecting babies from poisoning themselves, as they might do if they readily ate anything and everything. Parents can find this fussiness about food very frustrating and many worry unnecessarily, as almost all babies grow out of the fussy phase in time. Weight gain in babies over 12 months of age is lower than before 12 months and most babies eat less than their parents expect.

To ensure that babies receive all the nutrients they need from the small amounts of food they eat, they should only be offered nutritious foods. Each day they should be offered a variety of foods from the five food groups:

1 *bread, rice, potatoes, pasta and other starchy foods – serve them as part of each meal and some snacks*
2 *fruit and vegetables – serve them as part of each meal and some snacks*
3 *milk, cheese and yogurt – offer these three times each day*
4 *meat, fish, eggs, nuts and pulses – these are the best source of iron and should be offered twice a day, or three times a day for vegetarian babies*
5 *foods high in fat and/or sugar – offer these in very small quantities in addition to the other food groups, not instead of them.*

10 Only got ten minutes?

Your baby only needs breast milk or formula milk up until four to six months of age. Breast milk is preferable because it protects against illness which formula milk does not. Babies should start to be weaned onto solid food by six months. They all develop at different rates, and while some can wait until just before six months others will be ready sooner. No weaning should begin before four months, and if a mother is breastfeeding during weaning onto solid food, the risk of childhood diabetes and some food allergies is reduced.

Weaning is a learning process – babies need to be offered new tastes and textures so that they have the opportunity to learn to like the new tastes and to manage new textures. Babies usually begin on puréed food or well-mashed food and, once they have mastered this texture, they should be offered thicker mashed food with soft finger foods and then mashed food with soft lumps. From nine months they should be offered minced and chopped food with harder finger foods such as raw apple and carrot. As they begin to eat more food their milk feeds should decrease in amount and number. By 11–12 months babies should be eating family foods with the rest of the family and having two or three milk feeds per day.

During your baby's second year he is likely to become more fussy about which foods he will eat. This is a natural stage of development, protecting babies from poisoning themselves, as they might do if they readily ate anything and everything. It is more evident in some babies than others, and some parents find this fussiness about food very frustrating. If parents understand why their baby is fussy, allow him to choose what he will eat, keep offering a wide variety of foods even when they are refused and eat with their baby as often as possible then, in time, their baby will grow out of this phase.

Weight gain in babies over 12 months of age is lower than before 12 months, and many parents are concerned that their baby is not eating enough. However, most babies are usually eating enough, as they need less food than most parents expect.

Babies benefit from a daily routine of meals and planned snacks, as they do not eat well when they are overtired or over-hungry. Babies over 12 months should be offered three meals and two or three snacks evenly spaced throughout the day. When babies do not eat well at one meal, parents should remove uneaten food and wait until the next planned meal or snack before offering food again.

In order to ensure that babies receive adequate nutrients from the small amount of food they eat, they should only be offered nutritious foods. Their meals and snacks should be made up from a variety of foods from the five food groups:

1 *bread, rice, potatoes, pasta and other starchy foods – serve them as part of each meal and some snacks*
2 *fruit and vegetables – serve them as part of each meal and some snacks*
3 *milk, cheese and yogurt – offer these three times each day*
4 *meat, fish, eggs, nuts and pulses – these are the best source of iron and should be offered twice a day, or three times a day for vegetarian babies*
5 *foods high in fat and/or sugar – offer these in very small quantities in addition to the other food groups, not instead of them.*

In addition, all babies should take a vitamin supplement of vitamins A and D each day, as most babies do not get enough of these two vitamins from their food. Vitamin A is important for the immune system and vitamin D is key for bone development and to prevent rickets. Babies should begin this supplement at about six months of age. Babies drinking formula milk can delay this until they have reduced their formula intake to less than 500 ml/17 fl oz a day, as formula milks are fortified with these vitamins whereas breast milk and cows' milk are not.

To prevent dental caries babies should only be offered sweet food up to four times per day, and acidic drinks, such as fruit juices, squashes and other sweet drinks, should only be given occasionally and only at mealtimes. The safest drinks between meals are water and milk.

Introduction

As a new mother, the responsibility of feeding your baby to make sure that he/she survives and grows can seem overwhelming. You may receive lots of well-intentioned advice, but some of it may be conflicting. And there may be days when you despair and think you may never get it right. Just remember that there isn't only one right way to feed your baby – you, your baby and your lifestyle will determine what suits you both best.

In this book I have attempted to explain what is important and why. If you understand the process of how your baby will learn to eat and drink and learn to like and enjoy the food and meals you give him/her, then the two of you together should be able to find a way to achieve this.

I have included some sample routines, menu plans and recipes, but these are not for you to follow rigidly – use them as a guide to what your baby needs and what has worked for many other families.

There is so much more to feeding than just providing your baby with nutrients: there is the joy of watching your baby learn, develop and progress; and the love and trust that you give and receive at each feeding experience. Try to make each meal a pleasant time for you both, something that you both enjoy and look forward to. Always smile and praise your baby for eating well, but remember to let him/her decide how much he/she eats or drinks – your baby knows much better than you do how much he/she needs at each feed and meal.

To make for easy reading, I have used he and him throughout this book rather than write he/she and him/her repeatedly. However, this book applies to baby girls just as much as to boys.

Enjoy feeding your baby.
Judy More

1

Milk-feeding in the first
few months

In this chapter you will learn:
- *the health benefits of breastfeeding*
- *how to solve problems with breastfeeding*
- *how to choose an infant formula for your baby*
- *the benefits of having a feeding routine*
- *how to deal with common feeding problems in young babies.*

All your baby needs for about the first six months is breast milk
or formula milk. Either milk will provide most babies with all
their nutritional needs over this time. Breast milk has clear health
benefits for you and your baby but there are many reasons why
some mothers choose to use formula milk instead or a mixture of
both breast milk and formula milk. Whichever way you feed, as
long as you use either breast milk or formula milk for all milk-feeds
up to your baby's first birthday you will be giving him the nutrients
he needs to continue growing and developing.

Choosing between breastfeeding and
formula milk

There are several reasons why breast milk is considered preferable
to formula milk and even a short period of breastfeeding will
benefit you and your baby.

Health benefits of breastfeeding for your baby:

▶ *Boosting immunity: Your baby receives antibodies in your milk which help him fight off viral and bacterial infections that may be present in the environment you are both living in. He is therefore less likely to become ill with other infections such as ear infections and colds which can make a baby very uncomfortable, clingy and demanding of comfort and attention.*

▶ *He is less likely to get stomach upsets, diarrhoea and gastroenteritis as there is no chance that the breast milk is contaminated. There is no preparation procedure where the bacterial contamination can occur.*

▶ *Lower risk of illness during childhood: Breastfed babies are less likely to get chest and ear infections as well as diseases like diabetes when they are older children. This also means less time trailing off to your GP or waiting around in an outpatients department in a hospital or having to cope with your child on a hospital ward.*

▶ *Breast milk contains all the nutrients your baby needs in the right quantity and in an easily absorbable form.*

▶ *The iron in breast milk is very low but it is in a form which makes it easily absorbed. In contrast, the iron in formula milk is more difficult to absorb so higher levels have to be added. The excess iron which is not absorbed from formula milk encourages the growth of bacteria in the intestines which is another reason why formula-fed babies are more likely to get gastroenteritis and diarrhoea.*

▶ *He is much less likely to become constipated.*

▶ *There may be further health benefits that have yet to be discovered.*

Health benefits of breastfeeding for the mother:

▶ *You will be reducing your risk of early breast or ovarian cancer and osteoporosis or brittle bone disease later in life (when you have gone through the menopause).*

▶ *You will lose the weight you put on during your pregnancy on your thighs and buttocks. You will have a speedier return to*

the pre-pregnancy figure as breastfeeding helps the womb to contract and also burns calories.
▶ You will delay the return of your menstrual cycle, thus reducing the likelihood of you becoming pregnant again while your new baby is still very young. However, it is not a 100 per cent effective form of contraception so you should talk to your doctor about contraception.

Other factors to consider:

▶ *Convenience: Breast milk is always ready and at the right temperature. There are no bottles and teats to be sterilized. There are no feeds to make up and heat or cool to just the right temperature when your baby is screaming for a feed. You can begin feeding him within a few seconds.*
▶ *Mother's time: Feeding a baby is time-consuming and the mother is the only person who can breastfeed her baby unless expressed milk is used. Feeds can take up to an hour and there can be six or more each day in the first few weeks. However, time invested now in breastfeeding may save you time later on as breastfed babies are less likely to become ill. An ill baby is very demanding of time – he cries and is clingy and needs comforting.*
▶ *Cost: Breastfeeding is free compared to the cost of formula milk, bottles, teats and sterilizing equipment.*
▶ *Anxiety: There is no way of knowing how much milk your baby has drunk and some new mothers can become very anxious about this. Many mothers give up breastfeeding because they perceive they are not producing enough milk. With a bottle the volume drunk is easy to see and this can be reassuring.*
▶ *Commitment: not everyone finds breastfeeding natural or easy and many mothers only manage it with some help and support.*
▶ *Comfort: It can be uncomfortable when breasts are full of milk and your baby sleeps for longer than expected. Sometimes breasts leak milk, but breast pads inside your bra will prevent this showing on your clothes.*

- *There can be some pain when your baby begins feeding. This is more frequent if your baby is not attached properly. If this happens you will need to ask a midwife or breastfeeding counsellor to show you how to latch him on properly so that breastfeeding is more comfortable.*
- *Some mothers develop an infection called mastitis which causes painful, inflamed breasts. Others may experience lumps in the breast caused by blocked milk ducts. Both conditions can be treated, for example, by changing breastfeeding position. Women with severe mastitis may need antibiotics.*

Insight

Like a lot of mothers, I chose breastfeeding for the convenience of being able to begin feeding my babies quickly when they woke screaming with hunger, rather than have to fiddle about making up a feed in a sterilized bottle. However, significantly reducing the risk of having a sick baby is also a big motivation for most parents.

Breastfeeding in the first few days – what to expect

Your midwife will help you put your baby to your breast soon after he is born. Some babies don't appear to do anything while others may suck a little. It does help some babies get used to feeding.

Your baby will probably be sleepy after being born but next time he wakes give him a cuddle, talk to him and offer him a breastfeed.

The milk you make in the first few days is called colostrum and can be quite yellow or even orange. Colostrum is high in protein and anti-infective agents which build up your baby's immune system. Babies only take small amounts of colostrum and feed infrequently in the first two days. They sometimes sleep for long periods. They all lose some weight and this is normal and is now thought to be an important part of their development, protecting them from obesity and heart disease later in life.

Both you and your baby need to learn how to breastfeed. It is best to have contact details for help before your baby is born so that you can get the help and reassurance you need as soon as you feel it is not going as you would like or expect. The most common problem may be latching your baby onto your breast. If this isn't right you may find feeding hurts. Ask for a midwife or breastfeeding counsellor to watch you feeding so that they can teach you and your baby how to latch on correctly.

Many mothers who give up on breastfeeding say they would have liked to have breastfed for longer. It is important to have some backup help ready and easy to access.

When not to breastfeed

There are only two reasons why you would be advised not to breastfeed. These are if you are HIV positive or if you take certain drugs which could pass into your milk and affect the baby. Check with your GP or pharmacist about the safety of any drugs or supplements you are considering using while you are breastfeeding.

Establishing a feeding session routine

Use these first few feeds to develop a routine to the feeding session so that your baby knows what to expect at each feed.

Sample routine:

1 *When he wakes and cries, pick him up and feed from one breast until he is satisfied and comes off the breast by himself or falls asleep.*
2 *Cuddle him upright to bring up any wind and then change his nappy which will wake him up.*

3 *Offer the other breast and allow him to feed as long as he likes. He may fall asleep as he finishes.*

4 *Cuddle him upright again for a while as he may bring up some more wind.*

5 *Pop him back into bed and relax and look after yourself until the next feed is demanded.*

6 *Alternate the breast that you offer first at each feed so that you begin feeding on the breast which was offered second at the previous feed.*

Whatever your routine, stick to it – babies like routine and feel secure when they know what to expect.

Insight

I used this routine and it worked like a dream for me.
But you should decide how you want the feeding routine to be for you.

After about two to three days your breasts will suddenly seem to increase in size and you may feel some breast discomfort. The small volumes of colostrum are changing into the larger volumes of milk that your baby now needs. As this happens your baby will begin to demand feeds very frequently and you may be in for a very busy and uncomfortable 24 hours. Make sure that you have no other duties or responsibilities other than to your new baby for that day and arrange for someone to provide you with meals and drinks and cheerful company. In between feeds, eat and drink yourself, relax and try to sleep.

Your baby may demand feeds every two hours throughout this 24 hours, so it will be very time-consuming for you. However, your baby is determining the amount of milk he needs and your breasts are adapting to produce the amounts your baby demands. Keep to the feeding routine you have decided on and remind yourself that it will all be more comfortable tomorrow. Within a couple of days you will be producing only the amount of milk your baby is demanding and your breasts will feel comfortable again.

Over the next few days your baby will feed less and less frequently and take more milk at each feed. Keep your feeding session routine going and you may find by the end of the first week you have a baby who is demanding feeds about every three to four hours and sleeping most of the rest of the time. Some babies prefer smaller feeds and may continue to demand smaller more frequent feeds. However, as they grow this frequency will usually decrease.

Supply meeting baby's demands

From now on your baby will control the amount of milk produced as your breasts will produce the amount he regularly drinks. There may be times when your baby is in a growth spurt and he will be hungrier and want more. During this time he may demand feeds more frequently to satisfy his hunger but as you produce more in response to his demands he will soon revert back to his previous routine.

Premature babies

Babies who are very premature may have to be fed via a tube into their stomach via their mouth or nose for a while. Breast milk is the best nutrition for a premature baby and the hospital staff can show you how to express milk for your baby so that he will still be having your milk even though it is via a tube. As your baby gets older and grows he will be able to begin feeding directly from you.

Breastfeeding twins

Feeding twins is time-consuming, so plan to have some extra help for your other responsibilities such as looking after older children, laundry, shopping and cooking.

Many mothers successfully, exclusively breastfeed twins. Once again a routine is important and your twins will settle into this once you have an established pattern. It is very important that you eat and drink well as you will need some extra nutrients, calories and fluid.

Putting your babies to the breast within the first hour or two after birth helps in establishing breastfeeding but isn't essential. The support of a feeding counsellor or advice from a mother who's done it herself will be extremely useful for you.

At first many mothers find it easiest to feed their babies one at a time. The first fed is the twin who wakes first at the beginning of the day and who may well continue to be the first throughout that day. The next day it may be the other twin who feeds first.

Once breastfeeding is well established, most mothers find that breastfeeding both twins simultaneously saves time. Each twin is offered one breast each at each feed. A stronger twin can stimulate the let-down reflex for a weaker twin. As the two breasts produce different quantities of milk it is best to alternate the breast that each twin feeds from.

Insight
A friend of mine exclusively breastfed her twins until weaning and said she was delighted to do it without having to fuss with bottles. She did have a lot of support to do laundry, shopping and other chores in the house.

Expressing milk

By expressing breast milk you can maintain the health benefits of exclusive breastfeeding even though you may be back at work or away from your baby for extended periods of time. It is best to wait until your breastfeeding is well established and you and your baby have a routine before expressing milk. This may take a few weeks.

If you express milk at the same time each day, your breasts will adjust and be ready to produce at that time each day. As with breastfeeding, routine is important.

You will need to buy bottles, teats and a set of sterilization equipment to sterilize them.

There are three ways you can express milk:

▶ *by hand*
▶ *using a hand pump*
▶ *using an electric pump.*

Ask a breastfeeding counsellor or your health visitor or midwife to advise you on how to express milk. It can be expressed directly into a sterilized bottle or into a special plastic bag. If you are going to use it within 48 hours then store it in the fridge. You need to freeze it as soon as possible if you are going to keep it for longer.

USING EXPRESSED BREAST MILK

Thaw the milk in the fridge so that it stays cold. Warm it up just prior to feeding by standing it in a jug of warm water. Using a microwave oven is not recommended as milk does not heat uniformly in a microwave and there may be hot spots which can burn your baby's mouth. Also, the milk carries on heating up after you have taken it out of the microwave oven. Whichever way you heat the milk always shake the milk to distribute the heat and then test the temperature by shaking a few drops onto your wrist. It should be about body temperature so should not feel warm or cold on your inside wrist.

What to eat and drink when breastfeeding

There is no need to eat for two while breastfeeding as you laid down a store of extra energy on your thighs and buttocks during your pregnancy. However, it is very important that you eat well to help you replenish your body stores of certain nutrients which will have been used up during your pregnancy. Base your eating on a variety of nutrient-rich foods by including foods from all the food groups below each day.

Foods to include:

▶ *Bread, potatoes and other cereals including pasta, rice, couscous, sweet potatoes, breakfast cereals, chapatti and foods made from flour such as crackers and crispbread. These foods give you energy along with vitamins, minerals and fibre and should make up the main part of each meal.*
▶ *Fruit and vegetables – aim to eat five or more portions per day by including them at each meal and some snacks. Fresh, frozen, tinned and dried are all included.*
▶ *Milk, yogurt and cheese are important sources of calcium – aim to have two to three portions each day. Low-fat products have just as much calcium so use these if you are concerned about your weight.*
▶ *Meat, fish, eggs, nuts and pulses provide protein, iron and zinc as well as other minerals and some vitamins. Include them twice a day – or three times per day if you are a vegetarian. Include some fish twice a week and have oily fish at least once a week for a good source of omega 3 long-chain fats which your baby's brain needs as it is developing.*

Only eat very small amounts of foods high in fat and sugar as these have less nutrients and too many of them may stop you losing the extra weight you have gained during pregnancy. Foods high in fat and sugar include oils, butter, margarine, cream, cakes, biscuits, ice cream, sweets, chocolate, and sweetened drinks and snack foods such as crisps.

SUPPLEMENTS TO TAKE: VITAMIN D

Many women, particularly those with dark or pigmented skins have low levels of vitamin D. Sunshine on our skin makes almost all our vitamin D as very few foods contain it. Because we spend much less time outside nowadays many people have low levels of vitamin D. Babies of mothers with low levels are at risk of poor bone formation and rickets.

Healthy Start Vitamins for Women provide ten micrograms of vitamin D, which is recommended for breastfeeding women. Other brands are available in pharmacies and on the internet. Choose Vitamin D3 rather than D2 which is the less active form.

Insight

It used to be difficult to find a supplement that contained only vitamin D but with the current emphasis on good bone health they are now more widely available. If your pharmacist doesn't usually stock them, ask him to order some in for you. Alternatively buy a reputable brand on-line.

Foods containing vitamin D

▶ *Oily fish.*
▶ *Margarines and a few breakfast cereals are fortified with it.*
▶ *Meat and eggs contain very small amounts.*

FOODS TO AVOID OR LIMIT

▶ *Avoid shark, swordfish and marlin. They are very large fish which live for many years and can accumulate high levels of mercury in their flesh.*
▶ *Limit oily fish to two servings per week. These fish are a very good source of omega 3 fats but their flesh may contain some toxins. The amount that would pass into the breast milk from two servings per week would be minimal and not a risk for your baby, however, it is best not to eat it more frequently than twice a week.*

▶ *Avoid or limit caffeine and alcohol – both pass through into breast milk so avoid these or limit them.*

Caffeine

There is no recommended safe limit for breastfeeding mothers but if your baby seems restless then cut back to 50–100 mg caffeine per day.

Caffeine content of drinks

Average cup instant coffee	75 mg
Average mug coffee	100 mg
Average cup brewed coffee	100 mg
Average cup tea	50 mg
Regular cola drink	up to 40 mg
Regular energy drink	up to 80 mg
Average cup cocoa	about 20 mg

Alcohol

If you do drink alcohol, keep to one unit of alcohol at a time and avoid it altogether if you will be feeding your baby within an hour or two.

Alcohol units

½ pint standard strength beer, lager or cider	1 unit
1 pub measure of spirits	1 unit
1 small glass wine	2 units

Feeding with formula milk

Most babies have some formula milk as it is the only alternative to breast milk that should be offered during their first year of life.

Infant formulas can be used from birth or at any time you decide to discontinue breastfeeding. They are manufactured to very strict standards set out by European laws and are based on the content of mature breast milk. The companies making infant formula are continually researching and developing milks so that they are as close to breast milk as is technologically and economically possible.

CHOOSING A FORMULA – ARE THEY DIFFERENT?

Because of the strict guidelines the milks are all very similar with only slight differences. There is generally no advantage for your baby in changing from one brand to another in the first six months unless your doctor advises a change to a more specialized milk if your baby has a medical condition.

Most formula milks are based on modified cows' milk with added nutrients. There are two main types: whey dominant and casein dominant.

Whey dominant formula milks suitable from birth

The protein in these milks is 60 per cent whey and 40 per cent casein which is similar to the whey-to-casein ratio in breast milk. A soft curd forms in the stomach.

Examples: Aptamil First
             Cow & Gate 1 first infant milk from newborn
             Hipp Organic First Infant Milk
             SMA 1 First Infant Milk

Casein dominant formula milk suitable from birth

The protein in these milks is 20 per cent whey and 80 per cent casein which is similar to that in cows' milk. They form a firmer curd in the stomach and this stays in the stomach for longer. Although some are called second milks there is no reason to change to them as your baby gets older as, apart from the protein ratio, they have the same nutritional content as the whey dominant milks.

Examples: Aptamil Hungry Baby
             Cow & Gate 2 infant milk for hungrier babies
             Hipp Organic Second Infant Milk
             SMA Extra Hungry

Should I use an organic formula?
An organic formula will be guaranteed to be free of pesticides
because of the strict criteria for organic milk production. The
regulations which govern non-organic formula are extremely strict
on pesticide content such that the difference between organic and
non-organic formula milks is now very little.

In non-organic formula milks:

▶ *most pesticides are banned and the milks must be tested to
   show that these pesticides are non-detectable*
▶ *certain pesticides which are considered safe are allowed but
   the maximum allowable content is extremely low.*

Modified formula milks suitable from birth
The range of formulas has increased in recent years to include some
that are slightly modified and are promoted as being more suitable
for certain common conditions.

Modified formula milks	
Modifications	**Examples**
Higher amounts of some nutrients for pre-term infants following hospital discharge	Nutriprem 2
Added constituents which thicken the milk in the baby's stomach and reduce regurgitation in babies with reflux	Enfamil AR SMA Staydown
With modified protein, modified fat and thickeners which may better suit some babies with colic symptoms	Aptamil Comfort
The milk sugar lactose is replaced by other sugars for babies with lactose intolerance	Enfamil Lactofree SMA LF

Choosing a formula milk for a baby at high risk of allergy
Babies who have a parent or a sibling who has an allergy or suffers with eczema, asthma or hay fever are at a higher risk of developing these conditions themselves. Ideally they should be exclusively breastfed to reduce the risk of developing an allergy.

If your baby is in this high-risk category and you wish to use a formula milk, then use one that is extensively hydrolysed, such as Nutramigen 1 (Mead Johnson) or Cow & Gate Pepti-Junior.

Insight
> You can order these milks from a pharmacist, but they are two or three times more expensive than normal formula based on cows' milk. Some babies refuse to drink them as they have an unusual taste.

Soy-based formula milks
The protein in these formulas is from soy beans rather than cows' milk and the carbohydrate is glucose rather than lactose. These are not recommended for infants under six months because there may be unknown consequences of their high phyto-oestrogen content on the development of young infants.

Examples: Infasoy
              SMA Wysoy
              Prosobee

Milks for infants based on goats' milk
In Europe, infant formula regulations only allow formula milks based on cows' milk protein or soya protein. Since March 2007, milks based on goats' milk protein and recommended as suitable for babies under 12 months (infants) can no longer be legally sold in the UK. However, they are still sold in other countries.

FOLLOW-ON FORMULAS

These are for babies over six months old. See Chapter 3.

SPECIALIZED INFANT FORMULAS

There are a range of formulas which can be prescribed for babies diagnosed with cows' milk protein intolerance, malabsorption, metabolic syndromes or certain diseases.

Examples: Elemental formulas
Extensively hydrolysed protein formulas – for babies with allergies
Formulas low in disaccharides and non-milk protein
Formulas with fat modified to be high in medium-chain triglycerides
High-energy formulas
Soya-based formulas

Alternative formulas for babies with allergies
A very small number of babies have an allergy to or do not tolerate normal formula milks.

Signs that your baby may be allergic or intolerant to normal formula milk are constipation, diarrhoea, eczema or poor weight gain.

It is best to discuss this with your health visitor, GP or a dietician before changing the formula. The alternative formulas that your baby can take are much more expensive but will be prescribed if a healthcare professional agrees that your baby may be allergic to the cows' milk protein in normal formulas. It is best to have professional advice on which is the best formula to try as an alternative.

The formula most likely to be prescribed is an extensively hydrolysed formula which contains proteins that have been broken down (hydrolysed) into smaller segments that are less likely to cause an allergic reaction. Although these formulas are less likely to cause an allergic reaction, some babies may refuse them due to their unusual taste. There are three types:

1 *Extensively hydrolysed formulas based on casein are the most broken down formulas (Nutramigen 1 – Mead Johnson).*
2 *Extensively hydrolysed formulas based on whey contain slightly larger protein segments but may be better tolerated in older babies due to their more acceptable taste (Cow & Gate Pepti-Junior).*
3 *Non-milk based extensively hydrolysed formulas are also available although they may not be suitable for certain religions, cultures or vegetarians as they are based on meat derivatives (Peptide – SHS, Prejomin – Milupa).*

Partially hydrolysed formulas should not be used for babies who are suspected of having a cows' milk allergy or intolerance. The larger segments of protein can cause the allergic symptoms to continue. These formulas are no longer sold in the UK but they are available in other countries.

Amino acid formula (NEOCATE – SHS) is based on free amino acids which are the simple building blocks that make up a protein and is highly unlikely to cause an allergic reaction. It can be prescribed for babies who do not tolerate an extensively hydrolysed formula or if an extensively hydrolysed formula is not appropriate.

Soya-based formulas are not recommended for babies with allergies to cows' milk protein as those infants are also likely to be allergic to soya protein.

Babies who react to cows' milk protein are highly likely to react to other mammalian milks such as goats' milk formula and sheep's milk.

Milks based on peas, oats, rice and other foods are not suitable for babies under 12 months as they do not have the appropriate levels of nutrients to support the rapid growth and development of babies.

Developing feeding routines

Whether you are breastfeeding or using formula milk it is ideal
to get into a daily routine as well as a routine each time you feed.
Babies thrive on a routine and knowing what to expect next.
Routine helps them to feel safely contained and cared for. By about
one to two weeks after your baby's birth you should begin to find
each day is more predictable. After a sleep your baby will wake
hungry and cry for your attention. When you pick him up he will
show you he is hungry and wants to be fed by moving his head
from side to side and opening his mouth – this is called the rooting
reflex. You should soon learn when your baby is telling you he
is hungry.

Each mother and baby will develop a routine to suit their needs.
Your baby will feed best if you follow his cues and feed him when
he is telling you he is hungry.

Feeding takes time but it is a good opportunity for cuddling your
baby and talking to him while he is feeding. He will be getting
to know you and learning all about you by watching your face,
listening to your voice and becoming accustomed to your smell.
Some babies will feed quickly and others may take longer. Try not
to hurry the feed because if he doesn't get as much as he wants he
will get hungry and demand feeds more frequently. Allow him to
take as much as he wants – he will let the nipple or teat fall out of
his mouth when he has had enough. Don't coerce him to take more
from a bottle just because there is some left. Give him a cuddle
upright to allow any air he may have swallowed with the feed to
escape and then change his nappy. Following this, offer him more
feed (the second breast for a breastfeeding mother) and again allow
him to take as much as he wants. He may not take any with this
second offer but most babies do.

If you are lucky you will settle into a routine with your baby
demanding a feed every three to four hours. During the first two

months it is important to feed during the night when your baby wakes as he will be hungry and needs food every few hours.

Typical feeding regimes in the first two months

Three-hourly feeds:
If he wakes at 6 a.m. he will feed at approximately 6 a.m., 9 a.m., 12 noon, 3 p.m., 6 p.m., 9 p.m., 12 midnight, 3 a.m.

Four-hourly feeds:
If he wakes at 6 a.m. he will feed at approximately 6 a.m., 10 a.m., 2 p.m., 6 p.m., 10 p.m., 2 a.m.

There will be times when this regime may be disrupted because he is growing faster and is hungrier. Breastfed babies in particular may demand feeds more frequently until the breasts have begun to produce more milk for him. If you are bottle-feeding and he is finishing every bottle then it is time to add in a couple more ounces so that he can drink more at each feed. After a couple of days he should revert to his regime of demanding feeds every few hours.

Crying is his way of telling you he is uncomfortable and as he gets older his discomfort may not always be hunger. He could be uncomfortable because he has a wet nappy, is too cold or too hot or simply bored and wants some company. Cuddling, talking and playing with him should comfort him if he is bored.

If you are misinterpreting his crying as hunger when he is not hungry you could be offering very small feeds too frequently. A baby who is breastfed too frequently and takes only small feeds will be drinking mainly the lower-energy milk produced at beginning of the feed that is watery, low in calories and thirst-quenching. During the feed the milk changes and becomes increasingly rich in fat and high in energy and calories. Babies who only take the lower-calorie early milk become hungry sooner and mothers find themselves in a cycle of feeding very frequently during the day. Formula milk has a standard calorie content that does not change throughout the feed.

Sleeping through the night without feeding

By about eight weeks of age it is usual for babies to sleep for six hours at night without waking for a feed, although many babies have managed to do this earlier and some will be a little later. Between the age of four to six months he may still need a feed during the night but will be extending his night-time sleep towards ten hours during the night.

You may have a period when he sleeps through some nights but not others. Once he has established a pattern of sleeping through without waking for a feed you can be confident that he is not getting hungry and does not need to be fed during the night. If he begins waking again it will be because his pattern of sleep is changing rather than he is hungry. Sleep in many ways is still a rather mysterious process, but what we do know is that it comprises many different stages and cycles. These stages are made up of different types of sleep, which occur in cyclical patterns during the night, interspersed with brief arousals when a baby may wake and cry for you. Comfort your baby and help him to resettle but do not begin to offer milk-feeds again as this may encourage a comfort habit which will become hard to break later on.

Many parents are tempted to begin weaning at this stage and ask if there are any specific foods which will make a baby sleep through the night. Beginning weaning early will not change the sleeping pattern.

Typical feeding regimes from two to six months

Three-hourly feeds:
If he wakes at 6 a.m. he will feed at approximately 6 a.m., 9 a.m., 12 noon, 3 p.m., 6 p.m., 9 p.m., 12 midnight.

Four-hourly feeds:
If he wakes at 6 a.m. he will feed at approximately 6 a.m., 10 a.m., 2 p.m., 6 p.m., 10 p.m.

Is your baby getting enough milk?

Without seeing how much a breastfed baby is drinking you may wonder if he is having enough.

Always allow your baby to decide when he has had enough. Let him feed for as long as he wants on both breasts at each feed and he will stop feeding when he is full.

You can be confident he is having enough if:

▶ *he seems contented*
▶ *he has several wet nappies each day*
▶ *he is awake and alert for some of the time each day (or night).*

If your baby is very sleepy and lethargic with no alert times during the day then he may not be getting enough milk and you should seek medical help.

Frequently weighing your baby is not recommended as weight varies a lot depending on whether a baby has just had a feed or passed urine or a stool. Your baby should be weighed when he has immunizations but other than this it is not necessary. You and your health visitor should be able to tell if he is contented and growing.

However, if you are worried you can ask your health visitor to weigh him, but not more frequently than every two weeks. Breastfed babies grow more slowly than formula-fed babies especially around four to six months. This is normal and may be an important part of their development which may protect them from obesity and long-term health problems such as heart disease in later life.

Expected weight gain: 0–3 months: about 200 g/week
(6–7 oz/week)
3–6 months: about 150 g/week
(4–5 oz/week)

EXTRA FLUIDS ARE NOT NEEDED

Breastfed babies do not need any extra fluid – no extra water or juice. Even in hot weather it is best to offer more breastfeeds if they seem thirsty. When thirsty and not hungry they will take a short breastfeed just drinking the fore milk – the watery lower-fat milk that is thirst-quenching.

In very hot weather, some bottle-fed babies may become thirsty in between their feeds. Formula feeds are a standard composition so a thirsty baby may not satisfy his extra thirst by having more milk. If you think he is thirsty try offering one to two ounces of cooled boiled water in a sterilized bottle.

Does he need vitamin supplements?

Most babies do not need to begin vitamin supplements until they are six months old. However, some babies who are born to mothers likely to have low vitamin D levels themselves will be born with very low stores of vitamin D and need to begin vitamin drops containing vitamins A and D from birth or one month. Mothers most at risk of having low vitamin D levels are:

- ▶ *those with dark pigmented skins*
- ▶ *those who spend little time outside, e.g. office and shop workers*
- ▶ *those who cover their skin when they are outside*
- ▶ *those living in northern areas of the UK.*

Coping with problems

A baby's stomach and intestines are developing and growing rapidly during early life. Some babies experience some discomfort because of this and may become unsettled or cry a lot. There is often very little that can be done except to comfort your baby by cuddling him.

Holding him upright half way through a feed will allow the escape of air that he may have swallowed while feeding.

POSSETING

Most babies will posset or bring up a little milk after a feed. This is because the valve at the top of the stomach has not yet matured and milk from the stomach is still able to escape back up from the stomach through the oesophagus and into the mouth. Babies who swallow a lot of air when feeding may posset more than those who feed efficiently and swallow less air. With time this valve will begin working more efficiently but this takes longer in some babies.

REFLUX

Babies who continue to have the problem of milk coming back up the oesophagus and sometimes into the mouth may be diagnosed as having reflux or gastro-oesophageal reflux, known by doctors as GOR. Babies suffer pain and discomfort with reflux and may become difficult or reluctant to feed well. Although they are hungry, soon after they begin feeding they will begin to experience pain. They often settle into a pattern of shorter but more frequent feeds which is more demanding for you to cope with.

Changing from one brand of feed to another will not help these babies but changing to a thickening feed, e.g. Enfamil AR or SMA Staydown may help. Breastfed babies can be given a thickener from a spoon just prior to the breastfeed. For most babies reflux improves at around three to six months. The situation sometimes improves when weaning onto solids begins.

For the few babies for whom the problem is severe or persists for a long time, a GP can prescribe anti-reflux medicines to reduce the pain and the reflux. Babies who have this condition severely may become difficult to feed as they get older as they now associate feeding with pain. You will need to take great care to make meals very positive experiences to improve your baby's attitude to food and feeding.

VOMITING

Almost all babies will have an occasional large vomit which may be caused by a variety of reasons. Babies who are encouraged to overfeed may vomit the excess feed. A baby who persistently vomits but is growing well does not have a problem.

Projectile vomiting is when the vomit comes up with such force that it shoots across the room. If this occurs with most feeds it is an indication of a serious condition called pyloric stenosis. It usually begins around two weeks of age and these babies should be seen by their GP and may require surgery.

COLIC

There is no agreement on what colic is or what causes it. Babies who cry excessively and for no apparent reason and seem inconsolable or in pain are often said to have colic. Some draw up their legs and scream with the pain. It is most common in babies from three weeks to three months old and occurs in about one in three babies. There are many remedies suggested and they may give a little relief for a few babies but more often babies grow out of it as they get older and their stomach and intestines grow bigger.

Colic makes for a distressing time for parents. Pharmacists sell a few remedies which may help some babies. Some mothers find a warm bath and gentle massage helps soothe their baby.

CONSTIPATION

Constipation is the difficult passage of hard stools. Breastfed babies rarely get this but it is quite common in formula-fed babies. It is most likely to occur if the feed is being made up incorrectly, particularly if the feed is made up too concentrated by adding too much powder. Check how you make the feeds. Count the number of scoops being added very carefully. Level the scoops off making sure you are not packing the powder down into the scoop.

CONCERNS ABOUT WEIGHT GAIN

After birth all babies will lose some weight. Some of this is various salts and fluid they no longer need once they are outside the womb. Breastfed babies lose more weight than formula-fed babies because colostrum, the early breast milk produced in the first two to three days, is lower in energy than formula milk. This weight loss is quite normal and experts now think it is an important part of your baby's development. The larger weight loss that breastfed babies experience may be one of the factors which reduce their tendency to become overweight or obese as children. Between day four and day seven your baby will begin to regain weight and most babies will have regained their birth weight between days seven and ten.

Occasionally babies who are not feeding adequately in the first week may not begin to regain their birth weight. They may become dehydrated and they will seem very tired, quite floppy and will not have a period of being alert each day. They may not always have a wet nappy when the nappy is changed. If your baby seems like this then there may be a problem with your feeding technique. Speak to your GP or health visitor urgently and if you are breastfeeding ask for a trained counsellor to help you make sure your baby is latching on properly. Dehydrated babies usually need a few days in hospital so that they can have some extra fluids via a tiny tube into one of their veins while both of you learn how to feed properly. When this happens to a breastfed baby it is easy for the mother to lose her confidence and be talked into changing to formula-feeding. However, as disappointed as you will be that breastfeeding your baby hasn't been successful, try to give yourself and your baby a little longer to get to know each other and learn how to make the breastfeeding work. Ask for help and have confidence that other mothers have been through this and were able to carry on fully breastfeeding once they had received the help and support they needed to get the technique correct.

After regaining their birth weight, babies gain weight at different rates but on average they gain about 200 g/7 oz per week in the first three months and then about 150 g/5 oz each week from three to six months.

It is not necessary to have your baby weighed frequently nor to monitor his weight carefully. If your baby is feeding well, having several wet nappies each day and is awake and alert for some time each day then you can be reassured that he is doing well. He will be weighed when you take him for his immunizations at two, three and four months of age.

Some mothers become very anxious about their baby's weight gain but frequent weighing can make you even more anxious. If you are breastfeeding this may affect your production of milk. If you are concerned and like the reassurance of having your baby weighed, every two weeks is the most frequently it should be done. If it is done more frequently than this the real weight gain will be masked by the amount of fluid your baby has in his stomach or bladder.

When your baby is measured, ask the health visitor or GP to plot the measurements carefully on the growth chart. Slower growth is no longer considered to be of such concern as babies who grow very quickly are at more risk of becoming overweight or obese as they get older.

Insight

Babies often cross centiles on their growth chart in the first six weeks, which is normal. From six weeks onwards, if your baby is crossing upwards on the centile charts, then you may be overfeeding him. This is possible even with breastfed babies.

10 THINGS TO REMEMBER

1 *Breastfeeding is better for your health and for your baby's health than feeding with formula milk.*

2 *Breastfed babies will take very small infrequent feeds for the first few days.*

3 *Around day three you will feel some discomfort in your breasts for about 24 hours as the colostrum changes to a higher volume of milk. Your baby will begin to feed more frequently at this time.*

4 *Babies feel safe and secure with a routine, so develop a feeding session routine so that your baby knows what to expect at each feed.*

5 *By the end of the first week or so your baby should have settled into a routine of demanding feeds about every three to four hours, but some babies take smaller feeds more frequently.*

6 *The only alternative milk to breast milk for babies up to six months is an infant formula. Those on the market are all made to strict regulations and there is not much difference between brands.*

7 *Breast milk or formula milk provides all the nutrients your baby needs for around six months.*

8 *Babies are getting enough milk if they seem contented, have several wet nappies each day and appear alert for some time each day.*

9 *If your baby has an allergy to normal formula milk your doctor will prescribe an extensively hydrolysed formula.*

10 *Most babies posset a little milk after feeds, but some babies have reflux and regurgitate more milk and cry with discomfort on feeding. Most babies grow out of this at around three months.*

2

Beginning solid foods by
six months

In this chapter you will learn:
- *how to begin weaning*
- *which foods and textures to begin with*
- *the skills babies need to learn to eat solid food*
- *which foods to avoid before six months*
- *which weaning foods to use for babies at high risk of allergy*
- *menu plans and recipes for first meals.*

Breast milk or infant formula will supply all the nutrients your baby needs for about the first six months of life. By six months babies need to begin to eat solid food as it will supply more nutrients in smaller volumes which will meet their increased needs for nutrients as they are growing bigger. Iron is the nutrient that is most critical at this age – the stores of iron that were built up in your baby's body before birth will have fallen to low levels by the time he is around six months old. Breast milk is too low in iron to provide enough now.

When is your baby ready to begin solids?

Many babies are happy to wait until close to six months to begin solid food and at this age they will learn the skills needed for eating solid food very quickly. Begin by the time he turns six months – do not leave it until after he is six months old. However, all babies develop at different rates and some babies will be ready before six months. No weaning should begin before four months because until that age babies' kidneys and digestive systems are not fully developed and ready for foods other than milk.

You will start to notice some of the developmental signs which will also indicate he is ready to begin learning to eat solid food. The developmental signs are:

▶ *He can sit up with support and control his head well – this means he will be unlikely to choke on solid food.*
▶ *He is investigating his environment by putting toys and other objects in his mouth – he will therefore be happy to try new sensations such as food in his mouth as well.*
▶ *He is watching you with interest when you eat.*
▶ *He seems not to be satisfied just with milk-feeds because you have offered larger milk-feeds but he is demanding them more often.*

Insight

Mothers of larger babies and male babies tend to start weaning earlier than mothers of smaller babies and female babies. This is probably because larger babies have progressed more quickly and are ready for more than milk at a slightly younger age. Baby boys grow at a slightly faster rate than baby girls and are probably ready for more than milk at a slightly younger age than girls.

WAKING AT NIGHT IS NOT NECESSARILY HUNGER

Beginning to wake during the night when he has been sleeping through is not usually a sign that your baby is hungry but may be caused by a change in babies' sleeping patterns around this age. Sleep oscillates between deep sleep and lighter sleep and also includes brief periods of arousal when babies may wake and cry for attention. They are not necessarily crying because they are hungry.

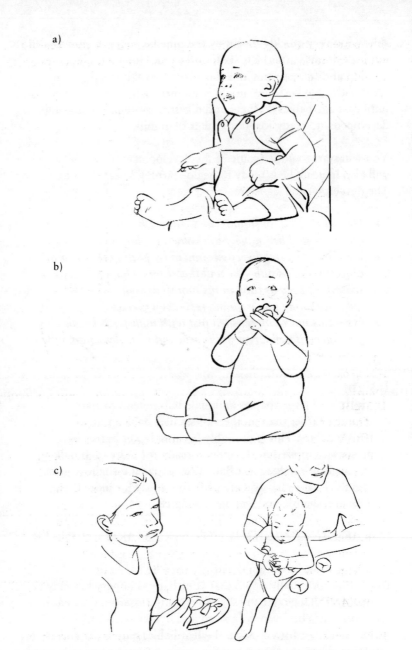

Figure 2.1 Developmental signs that your baby is ready to begin learning to eat solid food: a) he can sit up and control his head well; b) he puts toys and other objects in his mouth; c) he watches you eat with interest.

If you are in doubt about when to begin weaning ask your health visitor for advice. You could also give your baby a weaning spoon to hold and see if he is happy putting it into his mouth.

Figure 2.2 Give your baby a weaning spoon.

Insight

The age to begin weaning is a controversial topic now. The World Health Organisation recommends exclusive breastfeeding until six months to protect babies in developing countries from gastroenteritis. This is a risk for babies in those countries being bottle fed or eating solid food. In the UK no harm will come to your baby if you begin to wean earlier than six months. Unfortunately some websites and healthcare staff say that babies who begin weaning before six months are more likely to get infections and food allergies, but there is no evidence for this.

WEANING PREMATURE BABIES

Each premature baby needs to be considered individually when it comes to deciding when to begin weaning. Because they were not in their mother's womb during the last few weeks of pregnancy they have not built up the stores of certain nutrients which term babies will have done. Milk alone will not be enough for premature babies until about four to six months after their estimated date of delivery (EDD). See Chapter 5 for more information.

Equipment needed to begin weaning

To begin weaning (taking food rather than just milk) you will need:

▶ *Shallow plastic weaning spoons – at least two. The plastic rounded spoons are best but a normal teaspoon can also be used.*
▶ *Small bowls – at least two – so that you can serve two different courses. Plastic bowls will not break when they are accidentally knocked onto the floor. One with a suction base to keep it stable on the highchair tray or table is a good idea as your baby will be moving his hands and arms around quite enthusiastically. Make sure it has nice smooth surfaces that can be kept scrupulously clean.*
▶ *Small saucepan with tight-fitting lid.*
▶ *Bowls to mash or mix in.*
▶ *Implements to purée food. This can be a liquidizer, a hand-held blender, a food mill or a baby mouli. Alternatively a sieve to push food through with the back of a spoon can be used.*
▶ *A sieve will be useful to push food through to make sure the first meals are very smooth.*
▶ *Ice cube trays for freezing batches of food and plastic bags in which to store the frozen food cubes.*
▶ *Bibs with plastic backing to keep your baby's clothes clean and dry.*
▶ *A plastic cup or beaker with a lid and free-flowing spout. Choose one with just a few holes in it. Do not use a cup with a valved spout that your baby has to suck on. You want him to learn to sip drinks rather than continue sucking which he is adept at already. Choose a cup with two handles which will*

be easier for your baby to learn to hold and control himself. The holes in the spout let your baby learn to drink without having to suck but only let a small amount of liquid through at a time so he isn't overwhelmed by a large flow of liquid. Later you will be able to help him learn to sip without using the lid.

▶ *A good stable highchair with a feeding tray. Babies over six months will sit in a highchair but younger babies may need more support to sit and a baby seat used for the car or a stroller may be more suitable. As soon as he can sit happily in the highchair use this for feeding as he will be able to see the food and learn about it by touching it. You will also be able to put finger foods on the tray for him to pick up himself.*

Figure 2.3 Make sure you have everything you'll need to begin weaning.

First tastes

WHICH FOODS TO START WITH?

At first he will only take very small quantities so mixing a little baby cereal with breast or formula milk is convenient. Alternatively some puréed vegetables or fruit thinned down with milk will do.

Babies do not need to begin on bland tastes and many find something with a different flavour more interesting. However, using a cereal with his usual milk will be fine for the first few meals as he will be learning to take food off a spoon which is quite different to sucking from a nipple or teat.

> **Foods to use for the first few tastes**
>
> ▶ *Baby cereals, e.g. baby rice or a porridge made from oats, ground rice, cornmeal, maize, millet or wheat.*
> ▶ *Puréed or well-mashed potato, sweet potato, carrot or parsnip or a mixture of vegetables.*
> ▶ *Puréed or well-mashed ripe fruit such as banana, pear, peach, mango or cooked apple.*

Insight

Which cereals to begin with? Mothers used to be warned not to give cereals containing gluten before six months. However, advice has recently changed as new evidence shows that it is best to begin giving your baby cereals containing gluten between four and seven months. This may reduce the risk of your baby having coeliac disease. Waiting until after seven months increases the risk. Continuing to breastfeed while you are weaning gives the best protection to your baby.

WHAT TEXTURE?

Mix the food and milk so that they are a little thicker than milk, rather like a runny yogurt.

WHEN TO TRY?

Choose a time of day when you are relaxed and you know your baby will be alert. Make sure you will not be interrupted.

Halfway through a milk-feed is a good time so that he is not ravenously hungry nor so full he is not interested in trying some food.

HOW SHOULD A BABY SIT?

It is important to keep him in an upright position during feeding so that he does not choke. His head and back should also be supported unless he can already sit by himself. Either sit him in a seat which supports his head and back or, if you prefer to hold him, support his head and back with one arm and keep him more upright than when he is drinking his milk-feeds.

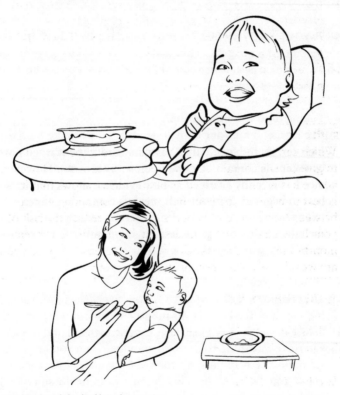

Figure 2.4 How your baby should sit when weaning.

HOW TO BEGIN

Begin with a smile! No matter how anxious you may feel, you are going to teach your baby to eat and enjoy solid food, one of life's great pleasures. As your baby can read the expressions on your face long before he can understand what you are saying, if you are anxious he will become aware of this and may become anxious also. Put a smile on your face and talk positively to him about the food. Let him dictate the pace and remember he has a lot to learn which will take time and patience and encouragement from you. Try to make every meal a pleasure for both of you.

Skills your baby needs to learn in the first few meals

At first, while he is learning new skills, he may take very little – just one or two teaspoons.

▶ **Taking food from the spoon**
  The first skill for your baby to learn is how to take food off a spoon. By the time babies are close to six months most will be exploring objects by putting them in their mouths. Some mothers give their baby the small weaning spoon to play with for a few days before the first meal so that it does not feel strange in their mouth. Half fill a plastic weaning spoon with the fairly runny first purée and slightly tip it into your baby's mouth allowing him to suck it off.

▶ **Using his tongue**
  The second skill he will learn is how to get the food from the spoon to the back of his mouth. When babies suck at the breast or bottle they push their tongue forward and the milk squirts towards the back of the mouth. When you first give solid food he may push his tongue forward and the food will come straight back out. This doesn't mean he doesn't like the food it just means he needs to try different tongue movements to find out which one will move the food to the back of his mouth. It may take several attempts for him to realize that by not pushing the tongue forward the food will stay in the mouth. Eventually he will also learn how to move the food to the back of his mouth to be swallowed.

To learn these skills he needs time, patience and a smiling face encouraging him. Generally babies who begin weaning closer to six months, rather than four months, will progress much more quickly. Remember that babies learn by watching others so make sure he has opportunities to see you and others eating.

How much food to offer

Don't worry how much he actually eats in the first few days as he will still be getting all his nutrients and energy from milk. Keep trying solids once a day, every day, so that it becomes part of the routine. Just as you have to keep practising when learning to ride a bicycle, babies need to keep trying to learn to eat more solid food. Practice makes perfect!

Some babies master these skills very quickly, others take longer. Be guided by your baby and go at his pace. If he finishes all the food you offer, mix up a larger quantity the next day.

Make sure the meal is a pleasant experience for you both and finish when he indicates he has had enough. Don't extend the meal to try and get him to finish all the food you have prepared. Always respect his decision that he has had enough so that he enjoys the meal experience and doesn't feel pressured to eat more than he wants to.

TELLING YOU HE HAS HAD ENOUGH FOOD

It is very important to try to read the signals your baby is giving you. If your baby opens his mouth he is ready for more food. If he closes his mouth or turns his head away he is telling you he has had enough practice at eating. He may even put his hand in front of his mouth.

Insight

I remember the temptation to encourage and cajole my babies to eat more of the food I had lovingly prepared for them.

(Contd)

I wanted them to eat it all. Try to remember it is a waste of everyone's time to persevere. There are more fun activities to enjoy together than trying to get one more teaspoon of food into his mouth which won't make much difference to his nutritional intake anyway.

Figure 2.5 Your baby is telling you he's happy to eat more when he opens his mouth as the spoon approaches.

Figure 2.6 Your baby is telling you he does not want any more food when he: keeps his mouth shut; turns his head away; puts his hand in front of his mouth.

TAKING MORE

Once your baby has mastered these skills he will begin to take a little more of the weaning foods and will realise that solid food will also satisfy his hunger. You can give the solids before the milk-feed now. Have the food ready for your baby when he re-opens his mouth. Hungry babies can get frustrated if they are fed slowly when they are used to drinking milk very quickly.

OFFER DIFFERENT FOODS AT DIFFERENT FEEDS

Choose another feed and offer a different food at that meal as well. For example, give cereal mixed with milk at one feed and puréed vegetables at the second feed. When you have both mastered this, try some puréed fruit at a third feed each day.

Daily plan for first meals

6 a.m.	Milk-feed
10 a.m.	Baby cereal mixed with baby milk
	Milk-feed
2 p.m.	Puréed vegetables
	Milk-feed
6 p.m.	Puréed fruit
	Milk-feed
10 p.m.	Milk-feed

Learning to like new tastes

Babies are born with an inherent liking for sweet tastes. The sugar found in milk (lactose) imparts a sweet taste to both breast milk and formula milk. When you first mix a baby cereal with milk your baby will probably find very little difference in taste between that and his milk-feeds. However, when you introduce vegetables and fruit these tastes will be quite different. He may show some surprise at a different taste and screw his face up if he detects a bitter taste from the vegetables. He may even refuse to take more by turning his head away. Do not be put off by this reaction; he is just telling you this is a new taste for him. Just offer it again the next day or a couple of days later. He may only take one teaspoon at a time but each time you offer this food he will become more familiar with that taste and in this way he will learn to like it.

> **Insight**
> I always used to make vegetable purées with a combination of at least one sweeter vegetable such as carrot, parsnip or potato along with the more bitter tastes of cauliflower, broccoli or courgette. That way the bitter taste is minimized and more acceptable to babies tasting it for the first time.

Adding more nutritious foods

Vegetable and fruit purées are fairly low in energy (calories). As your baby begins to eat more than just a few teaspoons of food at each meal you need to increase the energy, protein and nutrient content of the meals. You do this by:

1 *adding meat, fish or pulses to the vegetable purées*
2 *mixing fruit with cereals, yogurts or milk puddings.*

These foods should be introduced to your baby's diet by around six months old at the latest, as they are good sources of protein, and meat, oily fish, pulses and cereals provide iron. This is the time when the iron stores your baby laid down before birth are running low and need replenishing. The iron in meat and oily fish is very well absorbed from the intestine. Vegetarian babies who rely on pulses and eggs as their main sources of iron should include a food high in vitamin C with every meal because vitamin C boosts iron absorption from vegetarian meals. Most vegetables contain vitamin C and potatoes, peppers and tomatoes are very rich sources. Meat, fish and pulses will also provide other nutrients such as more B vitamins and zinc.

If you are using commercial baby foods change to those containing some meat, fish or pulses. Alternatively you could add a little puréed meat, fish or pulses yourself to the jars of vegetables you may have bought.

Insight

I would often keep a small amount of cooked meat from my dinner in the fridge and then the next day purée it into freshly steamed vegetables for my baby's dinner.

Foods to avoid

Honey should be avoided until one year because it can cause severe food poisoning in babies. Sugar should only be used sparingly to reduce the tartness of fruits. Salt should never be added to baby food but you can use herbs or mild spices to add flavour.

Insight

Previously parents were advised to avoid fish, eggs and cereals with gluten before six months. Evidence now shows that babies do not need to avoid any foods before six months to prevent allergies.

Weaning for babies at risk of developing allergies

Babies whose mother, father, brother or sister has asthma, eczema, hay fever or a food allergy are at a higher risk of developing an allergic disease themselves. Only very few of such babies will be allergic to certain foods. If you are still breastfeeding then keep breastfeeding while you wean as this reduces the risk of your baby becoming allergic to foods.

If your baby is at risk of allergy then only use foods very unlikely to cause an allergic reaction as the first weaning foods. These include:

▶ *rice*
▶ *potatoes*
▶ *root and green vegetables*
▶ *apples*
▶ *pears*
▶ *banana*
▶ *stone fruit such as peaches and apricots.*

When your baby is ready to begin meat, introduce lamb and beef as first meats.

You can introduce any of the pulses.

There is no evidence that introducing after a certain age the foods likely to cause allergic reactions prevents the allergy. Whenever you begin, introduce them one at a time so that it is easy to identify which, if any, causes a reaction. The foods most likely to cause a reaction are:

▶ *Food based on cows' milk – yogurt, fromage frais, cheese or cows' milk in a food. If you have already been using a formula milk then your baby will already have been introduced to cows' milk proteins and is unlikely to show a reaction when you begin using yogurt, cheese and fromage frais in his weaning foods.*

- ▶ *Eggs – make sure they are well cooked.*
- ▶ *Fish and shellfish – well cooked.*
- ▶ *Tree nuts – ground or as nut butter, e.g. ground almonds – but no peanuts.*
- ▶ *Wheat – breads, pasta, and foods containing wheat flour.*
- ▶ *Celery.*
- ▶ *Foods containing soy.*
- ▶ *Sesame seeds.*
- ▶ *Mustard seeds.*
- ▶ *Foods containing sulphites.*

Insight

There is a lot of research ongoing in this area involving families that have these allergic responses to certain foods. The early indications are that there is no need to delay introducing any foods. If your baby is going to react to a food then the age that he first eats it doesn't seem to make any difference. But only about one in 12 babies reacts to food, and for the most part the reaction is very mild.

Menu plans

FOR FIRST MEALS

	Day 1	Day 2	Day 3
Before 10 a.m. feed	Baby rice with milk	Porridge with milk	Wheat cereal with milk
Before 2 p.m. feed	Puréed or well-mashed potato and carrot	Puréed or well-mashed sweet potato and cauliflower	Puréed or well-mashed parsnip and broccoli
Before 6 p.m. feed	Puréed or well-mashed cooked apple	Puréed or well-mashed peach	Puréed or well-mashed avocado

FOR MORE NUTRITIOUS MEALS

	Day 1	Day 2	Day 3
Before 10 a.m. feed	Baby rice with puréed pear and milk	Porridge with puréed or well-mashed banana and milk	Wheat cereal with puréed cooked apple and milk
Before 2 p.m. feed	Puréed lamb with spinach and sweet potato	Puréed or well-mashed lentils with carrot and coriander	Puréed beef with potato, broccoli and red pepper
Before 6 p.m. feed	Puréed or well-mashed mango and yogurt	Puréed or well-mashed apple and pear	Puréed or well-mashed peach and apricot

Recipes for preparing first puréed meals

1 BREAKFAST CEREALS

There are a variety of dried baby cereals which can be quickly mixed with formula milk or expressed breast milk. Follow the instructions on the packet for quantities to mix. Wheat biscuit cereals can also be mixed with milk. Porridge, ground rice and millet make very economical baby cereals for your baby to start on.

Oat porridge
2 tbsp porridge oats
75 ml/2½ fl oz water
75 ml/2½ fl oz formula milk or cows' milk

Put the porridge oats into a small pan with the water and milk. Bring to the boil and simmer gently until the mixture thickens, which will take about five minutes. Take out a small portion and allow to cool. It will thicken a little more. Thin it down to the required consistency

with some puréed fruit, expressed breast milk or formula milk.
Freeze the remainder in an ice cube tray for other days.

You can also make this in a microwave by putting the ingredients
in a wide bowl and cooking uncovered on full power for about
three minutes. Stir well to make sure the heat is evenly distributed
and allow to stand for a few minutes to cool to a suitable
temperature for feeding to your baby.

Makes 6–8 servings.

Ground rice or millet breakfast cereal
1 tbsp ground rice or millet flakes
150 ml/¼ pint water or milk formula

Put the ground rice or millet flakes into a small pan with the water
or formula milk. Stir to disperse any lumps. Bring to the boil and
simmer gently until the mixture thickens, which will take about
five minutes. Take out a portion and allow to cool. It will thicken
a little more. Thin down to the required consistency with some
puréed fruit, expressed breast milk or formula milk.

Makes 6–8 servings.

2 SIMPLE VEGETABLE PURÉES

Simple potato purées
Potato and sweet potato both make suitable first purées. You can
steam the potato rather than boiling it.

1 medium potato or small sweet potato (about 100 g/3½ oz),
    peeled and diced
100 ml/3½ fl oz water
Expressed breast milk or formula milk

Put water into a small pan and bring to the boil. Add the potato
and cover with a tight-fitting lid. Bring back to the boil and simmer
over a low heat for about ten minutes until tender. Check to make
sure the water does not boil away and add a little more if necessary.

Purée the potato with the remaining water until smooth with no lumps. Take out one portion and freeze the other portions. Add expressed breast milk or infant formula to make the purée fairly runny.

Makes 12 servings.

3 COMBINED VEGETABLE PURÉES

Potatoes have more calories than other vegetables due to their high starch content. By mixing potatoes with other vegetables you have the ideal combination of calories and new flavours for your baby to enjoy.

Potato and carrot purée
Use this recipe for a combination of potato with other soft vegetables, e.g. broccoli, cauliflower, parsnip, butternut squash, swede, courgette and celeriac.

1 medium potato, peeled and diced
1 medium carrot, peeled and diced
100 ml/3½ fl oz water
Expressed breast milk or formula milk

Put water into a small pan and bring to the boil. Add the potato and carrot and cover with a tight-fitting lid. Bring back to the boil and simmer over a low heat for about ten minutes until both vegetables are tender. Purée the vegetables together with the remaining water until smooth with no lumps.

Makes 12 servings.

Sweet potato and cauliflower purée
This combination of these two vegetables is rich in beta carotene and introduces a new vegetable taste.

175 g/6 oz sweet potato, peeled and diced
120 g/4 oz cauliflower florets
100 ml/3½ fl oz water
Expressed breast milk or formula milk

Put water into a small saucepan and bring to the boil. Add the sweet potato cubes and pop the cauliflower florets on top. Cover with a tight-fitting lid and bring back to the boil. Simmer gently for about ten minutes until both vegetables are tender. Check to make sure the water does not boil away and add a little more if necessary. Purée vegetables and remaining water until smooth with no lumps. Take out one portion and freeze the rest. Add in expressed breast milk or formula milk until the purée is the right consistency.

Makes 12 servings/meals.

Parsnip and broccoli purée
1 medium parsnip (100 g/3½ oz), peeled and diced
120 g/4 oz cauliflower florets
100 ml/3½ fl oz water
Expressed breast milk or formula milk

Put the water in a small pan and bring to the boil. Add the parsnip cubes and put the broccoli florets on top. Cover with a tight-fitting lid. Bring back to the boil and simmer gently for about 15 minutes until they are tender. Check to make sure the water does not boil away and add a little more if necessary. Purée the vegetables with the remaining water until smooth with no lumps. Take out one portion and freeze the others. Add in expressed breast milk or formula milk to thin down if necessary.

Makes 6–7 servings.

4 SIMPLE COOKED FRUIT PURÉES

Apple purée
Use English apples such as Jonagold, Elstar, Russet and Cox for a sweet, non-tart taste.

1 sweet dessert apple, peeled and cored
1 tbsp water
Expressed breast milk or infant formula

Dice the apple and put into a small pan with the water. Cover with a tight-fitting lid and bring to the boil. Simmer gently over a low heat for about seven minutes until tender. Purée with the remaining water. Press through a sieve if you need a smoother consistency. Take out one portion and freeze the rest. Thin down with expressed breast milk or formula milk if necessary.

Makes 4–6 servings/meals.

Apple and pear purée
Combining fruits will add variety to your baby's first meals. You can also make a purée with just pears.

1 sweet dessert apple, peeled and cored
1 very ripe medium pear, peeled and cored
2 tbsp water

Dice the apple and pear and put into a small saucepan with the water. Cover with a tight-fitting lid and bring to the boil. Simmer gently over a low heat for about ten minutes until very soft. Purée the fruits together with the remaining water. Press through a sieve if you need a smoother consistency. Add in expressed breast milk or infant formula, if necessary, to make a thinner consistency.

Makes 6–8 servings.

Peach and apricot purée
Make this in the summer when peaches are in season. Orange coloured fruits are bursting with carotenes. You can use ripe mangos as well as apricots or nectarines.

1 ripe peach, peeled, stoned and sliced
2 ripe apricots, peeled, stoned and sliced or 4 soft dried apricots
1 tbsp water

Put the fruit slices into a small pan with the water. Cover with a tight-fitting lid and bring to the boil. Simmer gently over a low heat for about five minutes until tender. If you use dried apricots leave in the saucepan for about 20 minutes before puréeing so they have time to soften. Purée the fruits together with the remaining water. Press through a sieve if you need a smoother consistency. Add in expressed breast milk or infant formula, if necessary, to make a thinner consistency.

Makes 4–6 servings.

5 FRESH FRUIT PURÉES

Many fruits, when ripe, do not need cooking and will purée easily. Try ripe peaches, pears, apricots, mangos, avocados and melons.

Peach purée
1 small ripe peach, peeled, stoned and diced

Mash the peach with a fork and purée. For a very smooth purée push through a sieve using the back of a spoon. Add expressed breast milk or infant formula to thin down if necessary.

Makes 1–2 servings.

Avocado purée
When ripe – just soft to touch – raw avocado will purée beautifully. You have to make the purée just before serving otherwise the avocado will discolour.

½ small ripe avocado, peeled and stoned

Mash the avocado with a fork and purée. For a very smooth purée push through a sieve using the back of a spoon. Add expressed breast milk or infant formula to thin down if necessary.

Makes 1–2 servings.

6 FRUIT AND YOGURT COMBINATIONS

Mixing equal quantities of any puréed fruit with plain yogurt will make a delicious pudding. The riper the fruit, the more naturally sweet the pudding will be.

Puréed mango and yogurt
¼ ripe mango, peeled, stoned and diced
4 tbsp plain yogurt

Purée the mango and mix with an equal quantity of plain yogurt.

Makes 2–4 servings.

7 MEAT AND VEGETABLE COMBINATIONS

You can begin to cook some meat with any combination of vegetables. Meat will usually take a little longer to cook than the vegetable but it is very quick if you, or your butcher, cut it into small pieces. Try using combinations of meat and vegetables that you like. To get a good balance of nutrients combine about one third meat, one third potato, rice or pasta and one third vegetables.

Beef with potato, broccoli and red pepper
Red meat is very rich in iron, zinc and other minerals that your baby needs now.

60 g/2 oz lean braising beef, cut into small cubes
½ medium potato (about 70 g/3 oz), peeled and diced
3 small florets broccoli (about 50 g/2 oz)
¼ red pepper (about 30 g)
100 ml/3½ fl oz water

Wash the vegetables and dice them. Pour the water into a small saucepan and bring to the boil. Add the beef and put the vegetables on top. Cover with a tight-fitting lid and simmer for about 15 minutes until the meat is cooked right through and the vegetables are soft. Purée with the remaining water until smooth. Take out one portion and freeze the rest. Add some cooled, boiled water if you would like a thinner purée.

Makes 4–6 servings.

Lamb with spinach and sweet potato
Lean lamb from a thin loin or chump chop (about 60 g/2 oz), cut into small cubes

⅓ medium sweet potato (about 70 g/3 oz), peeled and diced
40 g/1½ oz frozen spinach
100 ml/3½ fl oz water

Pour the water into a small pan and bring to the boil. Add the lamb and diced sweet potato. Cover with a tight-fitting lid and simmer for about 15 minutes until the meat is cooked right through. Add the frozen spinach and keep simmering until the spinach has completely thawed and is piping hot. Purée with the remaining water until smooth. Take out one portion and add some cooled, boiled water if you would like a thinner purée.

Makes 4–6 servings.

8 VEGETARIAN COMBINATIONS USING PULSES

Using pulses such as lentils will provide vegetable protein and iron. This iron is more difficult to absorb than the iron in meat but adding a food rich in vitamin C, such as tomato, will help absorb the iron from pulses.

Lentils with carrot and coriander
3 tbsp red lentils
½ medium potato (about 70 g/3 oz), peeled and diced
1 small carrot (about 60 g/2 oz), peeled and diced
½ tsp ground coriander

150 ml/¼ pint water
½ tsp tomato purée

Rinse the lentils thoroughly with water by putting them in a sieve
and immersing in a bowl of water. Remove them from the water
and drain. Put the lentils, diced vegetables, water and coriander
in a pan and cover with a tight-fitting lid. Bring to the boil and
simmer gently for about 20 minutes until vegetables are tender
and the lentils are soft. Add the tomato purée and mix together in
a blender until smooth. If the purée is too thick add some cooled,
boiled water to thin down.

Makes 6–8 servings.

10 THINGS TO REMEMBER

1 *You should begin weaning your baby by six months.*

2 *Babies develop at different rates, and while some are happy to wait until just before six months others may be ready sooner. You should not begin weaning before four months.*

3 *Parents should consider signs of readiness when deciding when to begin.*

4 *Waking at night is not necessarily a sign of hunger, as babies change their sleep patterns about this age and are more easily aroused and often wake spontaneously.*

5 *Smile and talk positively while you are feeding so that your baby understands that this is a pleasurable, fun activity and not something to be scared of, which he might assume if you are very anxious.*

6 *Your baby needs time and practice to learn a lot of new skills during the first few meals – he needs to learn to take food off the spoon and to use his tongue to push the food to the back of his mouth where he can swallow it. Some babies learn quickly; others take longer.*

7 *Start with just a teaspoon or two of smooth-consistency food once a day.*

8 *Offer different foods at two and then three meals as your baby becomes more adept at eating.*

9 *Babies can judge better than you when they have had enough to eat and they will signal this to you by keeping their mouth shut, turning their head away or putting their hand up in front of their mouth.*

10 *If you are still breastfeeding, carry on during weaning as this will reduce the risk of your baby developing food allergies.*

3

Moving on (six to nine months)

In this chapter you will learn:
- *how to change the texture of the food*
- *how to increase the variety of the food you offer*
- *how to involve your baby more in the meal*
- *how to teach your baby to sip from a cup*
- *how when to begin giving vitamin drops.*

Now your baby has mastered taking food off the spoon he is ready to eat more solids and begin trying different foods with different flavours and textures. Babies of this age are learning about their environment by putting objects and toys into their mouth and so they are also happy to try these new tastes and textures of food.

Most of their food and nutrients are still coming from their milk-feeds so they may not eat large quantities. As they do begin to eat more they will cut down the amount of milk they are drinking. Continue to allow them to decide how much they eat and drink. Coercing them to eat when they have shown they have had enough can turn the meal into a negative experience for them.

Introducing a variety of foods

Foods you can offer your six-month-old baby include:

▶ *all cereal foods and foods made with flours*
▶ *all fruits and vegetables*

- *all meats and poultry – use lean meat to increase the iron content and make sure they are always well cooked*
- *liver – but limit it to one small serving per week because it has very high levels of vitamin A*
- *all fish and shellfish – make sure they are all well cooked and always carefully flake fish to remove all bones*
- *eggs – make sure they are well cooked*
- *nuts – only use them ground or as nut butter, e.g. ground almonds and smooth peanut butter*
- *plain yogurt and fromage frais*
- *cheese*
- *herbs and mild spices.*

Insight

Some parents say they have delayed introducing these foods until their baby is older, but your baby can digest all these foods well before six months and there is no reason to delay offering them. In fact, recent research indicates that the earlier you introduce new tastes the more quickly your baby will accept them.

Foods to continue avoiding include:

- *honey – it may contain spores of botulism which can cause serious illness in babies under 12 months*
- *foods with added salt*
- *foods with added sugar unless it is a very small amount added to tart fruit to make it palatable*
- *unpasteurized soft cheeses*
- *hot spices such as chillies.*

Checking for allergic reactions to food

The first and second times you give the foods most likely to cause allergies keep a close eye on your baby just to make sure he doesn't react to these foods. Reactions are extremely rare but could require medical treatment.

If you are really anxious about giving your baby certain foods, remember that severe allergic reactions to food are extremely rare. But you could try first rubbing a little of the food on his skin to see if it causes redness or swelling. If not, then try a tiny amount on his lips and if all is well you can give him some to eat.

The foods most likely to cause allergic reactions are:

▶ *foods containing milk – yogurt, cheese, fromage frais – if you have not yet used a formula milk*
▶ *eggs*
▶ *fish and shellfish*
▶ *nuts – ground or as nut butter.*

Making purées thicker and introducing mashed food

The first, fairly runny foods your baby eats are quite low in nutrients and energy (calories) so you need to begin making them thicker and less watery. Do this progressively so that your baby learns to cope with thicker and thicker purées. As soon as he is managing thick purées begin mashing the food rather that puréeing. Meat may need to be puréed for a little longer than vegetables which mash more easily. Meat which is softer such as tender cuts and slowly cooked meat in stews and casseroles will mash quite easily. See the recipes at the end of this chapter for some ideas on slowly cooking meats.

Babies who begin weaning very close to the age of six months can be moved on to mashed food quite quickly. In fact, you may only need to use puréed food a few times to make sure he can take food from a spoon competently.

Insight

Many parents skip puréed foods and begin on well-mashed food. This is usually successful with babies who begin on solids closer to six months, but some babies may need to develop confidence with purées before they can be moved onto mashed food.

Making sure there is enough iron and that your baby learns to like high-iron foods

Iron is one of the key nutrients your baby now needs more of than milk alone can supply. Meat and oily fish are the best sources of iron for your baby as they contain iron in a readily absorbable form. It is called haem iron as it is attached to the haemoglobin molecule. The iron in all other foods is not attached to haemoglobin and is called non-haem iron. In this non-haem form, iron is less readily absorbed by your baby. However, some will be absorbed so it is important to include these foods. The foods with higher levels of non-haem iron are cereals fortified with iron, pulses, peas, green leafy vegetables and eggs. Fruit and other vegetables have smaller amounts. If a food rich in vitamin C is eaten with the non-haem iron the iron will be better absorbed.

Readily absorbed haem iron from:	Less readily absorbed non-haem iron from:
Beef and lamb	Breakfast cereals with added iron
Pork	Eggs
Poultry – more in dark meat (e.g. chicken legs and thighs)	Pulses (e.g. peas, beans, dhal and lentils)
Liver – this should be limited to just once per week because of the high levels of vitamin A	Green vegetables
Oily fish (e.g. mackerel, salmon, trout, sardines and tuna)	Bread

Include a food containing a good source of iron at most meals, for example:

Breakfast: Baby cereal that is fortified with iron or egg.
Lunch: Meat or pulses with vegetables.
Evening meal: Egg or oily fish, vegetables or fruit.

Your baby does not have to eat large amounts of high-iron foods at this age because if he is drinking formula milk he will be getting some iron from that. What is important is that you introduce high-iron foods now so that he becomes familiar them and learns to like them. In this way he will be happy to continue eating them as he gets older. This is particularly important in his second year when he is growing very rapidly and needs a lot of iron from his food. Iron deficiency anaemia is most common in 18–24 month olds (see page 213).

Introducing lumps to encourage chewing

You do not have to wait for your baby to have a mouth full of teeth before you introduce lumpy food. Babies' gums are quite hard and can squash soft lumps very well. It takes a while to learn to control lumps in the mouth so don't be surprised if the first few times they come back out – it doesn't mean your baby is refusing to eat lumpy foods. He has to learn to move his tongue from side to side to get the lumps in place between his gums.

You can make lumpy food by mashing the food but stopping before it becomes a smooth mash.

Begin giving lumps when he can sit upright by himself and has good head control. This way, if a lump isn't chewed enough he can cough it back into his mouth and chew it some more. Coughing back lumps, or gagging, is a normal part of learning how to eat so don't feel you need to clap him on his back or tip him upside down. This will give him a fright and could make him wary of eating foods with lumps.

CHOKING

There is always the possibility that any baby may choke so never leave him alone when he is eating or drinking. He will be choking if he is gagging repeatedly and is obviously unable to move a lump that has become stuck in his throat. If this happens then lift him gently and turn him upside down. The lump should dislodge by virtue of gravity. If it does not, then tap him on his back until it does dislodge. Although you may have been frightened by such an incidence just comfort your baby and reassure him everything is fine.

Some mothers delay introducing lumps because of the worry of choking. However, unless you give your baby the opportunity to try new textures, particularly lumps, you will not be giving him the chance to learn the skills needed to eat these foods. Babies not given the opportunity to learn to chew at this age are more likely to refuse lumps and lumpy food quite stubbornly when they are older.

Insight

Some parents stop giving lumps when their baby spits them out. However, babies who spit out lumps are just letting you know they need more practice with lumps before they can manage to chew and swallow them. This is all the more reason to keep giving them lumps.

Involve your baby as much as possible

At around six months your baby will begin to sit independently so should be happy sitting in a highchair and will be able to take more interest in his meals. Put the food you are feeding him on the tray so that he can see it.

As meals get bigger, the time taken to eat them will be longer. Some babies have a very short attention span and may get bored quite quickly unless you let them become more involved by allowing them to play with the food. Playing with food is an important part of learning about food and developing a positive attitude towards food. So wash or wipe your baby's hands before a meal and allow him to put his fingers into his food and make a mess. Feeling food around the outside of his mouth is also important so don't keep wiping it away during the meal.

CAN YOU COPE WITH THE MESS?

Some mothers find coping with this mess quite difficult. However, it is an important part of learning so try to allow the mess during the mealtimes and clean it all up when the meal is finished. Paper on the floor under the highchair may help to contain the mess so that it can be cleaned up quickly at the end of the meal.

Teaching a baby to eat and feed himself is a messy business which is difficult to accept for some new mothers. Trying to restrict the mess by not letting him become more involved in the meal may result in your baby eating less.

Begin with finger foods

At the same time as introducing lumps, give him some soft finger foods at each meal so that he can begin to learn to feed himself. This will give him practice at biting off small soft lumps and learning to control them in his mouth.

For finger food, use the same foods you are already feeding him. If you are cooking vegetables then take out a few pieces before you mash the rest. Similarly, if you are preparing fruit then cut a few slices for finger foods before mashing the rest. Alternatively you can roast a few vegetable sticks – see the recipe on page 76.

Put the finger foods on his feeding tray and he will soon learn to pick them up himself.

Soft fruit pieces, e.g. mango, melon, banana, peach, papaya
  and kiwi
Cooked vegetable sticks, e.g. carrot, green beans, courgette,
  potato and sweet potato
Roasted soft vegetable sticks, e.g. potato, sweet potato, parsnip,
  pepper, carrot, courgette
Cooked vegetable pieces, e.g. cauliflower and broccoli florets
Cooked pasta pieces
Crusts of toast
Cheese cubes

Weaning onto finger foods only
There is a fad at present for giving babies only finger foods as their
solid food. This has never been tested to make sure babies fed this way
get enough energy and nutrients. It is better for your baby to learn to
eat finger foods and mashed foods from a spoon at the same time.

Insight
I have seen several mothers who have given up on finger
foods only as they find their babies do not get enough to eat
when they are restricted to only finger foods. Some babies
begin demanding more milk feeds, which is a backwards step.

Figure 3.1 Give your baby some soft finger foods at the same time as beginning with lumpy foods.

Introducing sips of water in a feeding cup/beaker

As your baby takes more solid food which is thicker and less watery he may become thirsty with his meals. Offer sips of water from a feeding cup throughout the meal.

Water for your baby to drink does not need to be boiled first. Freshly drawn tap water or freshly opened bottled water in a clean cup is fine. However, if you are abroad and unsure about the quality of the local tap water or bottled water then boil it first and allow it to cool.

Choose a beaker that has a free-flow spout with just two or three small holes so that your baby can learn to sip the water. Do not use the beakers which have a valve mechanism as he will have to suck from this and this will delay him learning to sip fluids.

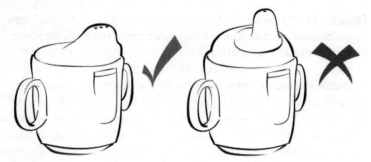

Figure 3.2 Choose a free-flow spout rather than one with a valve mechanism.

Sipping rather than sucking fluid is a new skill to learn so it will take quite a bit of practice before your baby can control the water flow himself. You will need to hold the cup yourself and gently tip it towards him so that very small amounts go into his mouth. With time he will try to hold it with you so that he learns about tipping it just a little to start the flow. A cup with two handles will be easier for him to hold and control.

Figure 3.3 *Sipping is a new skill to learn.*

Once he has mastered drinking from a spouted cup you can begin to use this rather than a bottle for milk-feeds. Aim to discontinue bottles by around one year of age.

If you have breastfed your baby up until now and you change to formula milk, offer it from a spouted cup rather than a bottle and you will not have to use bottles at all. Cups and spouts are easier to keep clean than bottles and teats and you will not need to sterilize a cup and spout if you are pouring the milk into it just before you offer it to your baby. Discard any milk he does not drink at that meal or feed.

Should I give fruit juice?

It is better to introduce water as a drink from this early age so that your baby doesn't always expect sweetened drinks. As you will now be offering fruit as a food you do not need to offer fruit juices. Vegetarian babies are the exception here as they may benefit from the extra vitamin C in fruit juice to help absorb the non-haem iron from a meal. However, as long as there is a fruit or vegetable high in vitamin C at each meal, vegetarian babies do not necessarily need fruit juice either.

If you do offer fruit juice always dilute it well and offer it from a cup, never from a bottle. Babies drink more slowly from a bottle and their teeth are therefore in contact with sugar and acid in the fruit juice for longer. This increases the likelihood of tooth decay.

Insight

Some mothers only give juice rather than water as juice has more flavour. Fortunately this attitude is changing. My babies were never offered juice and happily drank water throughout their childhood.

Continuing with bottle-feeds

If you are using bottles for milk-feeds you may find it more difficult to change to a cup for milk-feeds. However, make sure your baby gets used to a cup with water at mealtimes and you can then consider offering milk at the end of one of his meals in a cup rather than a bottle. If he accepts this at one feed, over time you can change to a cup at other feeds. You may find the last feed at bedtime the most difficult to change. It may be worth leaving this one in the bottle until he drops this feed altogether at around 12 months. You need to aim to have stopped using bottles with all other feeds by 12 months of age. After this age babies begin to associate the bottle with comfort and it will be harder to give up.

Insight

Both my babies moved onto milk in cups between about six and seven months, which meant I never had to use bottles.

Should I change to follow-on milk?

There are several follow-on milks available and they are marked as being suitable for babies from six months olds. You do not have to change to one at this age and can continue with breastfeeding or the formula milk that is suitable from birth and that you are already using.

Follow-on milks differ from formula milks suitable from birth in having higher amounts of protein and some vitamins and minerals – iron, zinc and vitamin D in particular. However, your baby will be getting more of these nutrients as he begins to eat more solid foods. If your baby is learning to eat well and you are including some foods with iron in either the haem or non-haem form at each meal then you do not need to use a follow-on formula. It is better to encourage your baby to eat a variety of foods rather than rely on his getting extra nutrients from fortified milks.

If you find your baby is very slow to accept solid food then you could discuss changing to a follow-on milk with your health visitor or doctor. There are several available:

Aptamil Follow-on Milk
Cow & Gate Follow-on Milk
Hipp Organic Follow-on Milk
SMA Follow-on Milk

Insight

There is also a follow-on 'Good night' milk that implies that your baby will sleep better through the night if this milk is given at the last feed of the day. Some of the lactose in this milk has been replaced with rice and other cereals, but there is no evidence that this makes babies more settled and more likely to sleep through the night.

Offer two courses to increase variety

Around seven to eight months, when your baby is eating small bowls of food, begin to offer two courses at the lunch and evening meals. This will give him a wider variety of foods but also make the meals more interesting for him. Make the first course a savoury course with meat or fish or egg or pulses combined with a starchy food and vegetables. Combine these foods together in roughly equal quantities so that you have about one third meat, fish, egg or pulses, one third starchy food such as potato, rice, pasta, bread or chapatti and one third vegetables.

Figure 3.4 Give equal quantities of meat/fish/pulses, starchy food and vegetables.

For the second course offer fruit, or a milk pudding, or a combination of both. A milk pudding could be a yogurt or fromage frais or a cooked milk pudding such as rice pudding or custard.

Continue to finish each meal by offering your baby a milk-feed. As he eats more at each meal you will notice he will begin to drink less milk. Eventually he may refuse his milk-feed altogether at his main meal as he is eating enough to satisfy his appetite.

Each time you introduce a new food he may show some surprise at the new taste. If it is a new vegetable he may screw up his face because of the bitterness. Do not insist on your baby eating more when he indicates he doesn't want any more. Offer the food again a few days later and he may be willing to have a larger helping. Each time you offer the food, he will become more familiar with the taste and texture. It doesn't matter how much he eats each time. After you have offered the food a few times he will learn to like it.

Make sure you offer different foods at each meal and choose those with plenty of flavour. Babies, like adults, can become bored with bland foods.

How long should mealtimes last?

It is important that you let your baby take as much solid food as he wishes and then finish the meal with a milk-feed. Do not rush the meal or extend it unnecessarily when he tells you he has had enough.

An average mealtime for this age is about 10–15 minutes. He will eat most of what he wants to eat fairly quickly. When he has had enough he will:

- ▶ *no longer open his mouth when you bring the spoon toward him*
- ▶ *turn his head away*
- ▶ *push the spoon away as you bring it towards him*
- ▶ *push the plate away.*

Offer the food only once or twice more to make sure he has had enough, but do not coerce him to eat more or play games to slip a spoonful into his mouth when he is unaware you are going to. It is important for babies to appreciate when they have had enough food and for you to respect that decision.

When he has had enough of the first course he may still be happy to try a second course. This will be new and interesting to him because there will be different flavours.

After each course praise him for eating well and take the uneaten food away with a smile. Never force feed. Always discard the uneaten food as it will now have some bacterial contamination and should not be offered again later.

Offer his usual milk-feed to finish the meal. If he has eaten a lot he may drink less milk than expected. Again, allow him to decide when he has had enough milk

If you are having your baby weighed frequently you will notice his weight gain is less from about six months. This is quite normal for all babies and the new growth charts are now based on breastfed babies and show the ideal growth pattern for all babies. If your baby seems content and is gaining some weight then you can be assured that he is having enough food and milk. If your baby begins to cross the centile lines upwards on his growth chart you may be encouraging him to have too much milk – this is more likely to happen with babies on formula milk, but breastfed babies can also be coerced to eat more than they need. Discuss it with your health visitor if you are worried.

Develop a routine around your baby's sleep pattern

Babies of this age need about 14 hours' sleep and this will probably be a night-time sleep of about 10–12 hours and two or three daytime naps. Fit in the meals and feeds around your baby's sleep pattern. He will enjoy feeding when he has recently woken up rather than just before he is due for another sleep and is very tired.

Keeping to a routine will make your baby feel safe and cared for. There is no need to wake him if on occasions he sleeps slightly longer. You can make the meals slightly later. He is growing while asleep and doesn't need to be woken to keep to a regimented routine.

Your routine may be something like:

AT SIX TO SEVEN MONTHS

On waking 6:30 a.m.–7 a.m.:	Breast or bottle-feed.
8 a.m. breakfast:	Baby cereal fortified with iron and mashed fruit and milk.
	Finger foods: soft fruit slices or toast crusts.
	Breast or bottle-feed.
10 a.m. sleep for about an hour	
12:00–1 p.m. lunch	Puréed meat or mashed fish or pulses with mashed potato or rice and with mashed vegetables.
	Finger foods: soft vegetable sticks.
	Milk-feed in a bottle or cup.
2:30 p.m. sleep for about an hour	
5 p.m. tea:	Mashed fruit and yogurt or milk pudding.
	Finger foods: soft fruit sticks.
	Breastfeed or cup of formula.
6:30 p.m. bath and bedtime routine	
7 p.m.:	Breastfeed or bottle of formula.
7:15 p.m. into bed	

AT EIGHT TO NINE MONTHS

On waking 6:30 a.m.–7 a.m.:	Breast or bottle-feed.
8 a.m. breakfast:	Baby cereal or porridge and mashed fruit and milk or egg with bread or toast.
	Finger foods: soft fruit slices or toast crusts.
	Breast or bottle-feed.

(Contd)

10 a.m. sleep for about an hour

12:00–1 p.m. lunch

First course: mashed meat or pulses with mashed potato or rice and with mashed vegetables.

Finger foods: soft vegetable sticks.

Second course: mashed fruit with milk-based pudding.

Finger foods: soft fruit slices.

Breastfeed or milk-feed in a bottle or cup.

2:30 p.m. sleep for about an hour

5 p.m. tea:

First course: mashed fish with mashed vegetables; or scrambled eggs with bread or toast; or pasta with cheese or vegetable sauce; or chapatti with mild curry.

Finger foods: soft vegetable sticks or cooked pasta pieces.

Second course: mashed fruit.

Finger foods: soft fruit slices.

Breastfeed or milk-feed in a bottle or cup.

6:30 p.m. bath and bedtime routine

7 p.m.: Breastfeed or bottle of formula.

7:15 p.m. into bed

Using commercial foods – how good are they?

Commercial baby foods are widely available and can be very convenient. However, they are not the same food as you eat as a family. The aim of weaning is to help your baby learn to like the taste of the foods you eat and the tastes you want him to eat as he grows up. So using commercial foods all the time will not allow him to learn to become familiar with those important tastes of your family food. However, there is room in any baby's eating pattern for some commercial foods especially when you are away from your home or rushed and it is more convenient to use them.

Commercial baby foods are made to strict criteria laid down by European legislation governing all the ingredients that can be added. There is a minimum amount of meat specified if the meat is named on the label: a minimum of eight to ten per cent of the weight of the food must be meat, which is quite low. Manufacturers tend to include only this minimum amount of meat to keep the cost down which makes the savoury foods quite low in iron. This is not a problem if you are only using them occasionally. However, if you are using them frequently then you could add some extra puréed meat to increase the amount of iron and other nutrients your baby gets from his savoury course.

Beginning vitamin drops

Most breastfed babies or babies who are being fed with breast milk and formula milk need to begin vitamin drops containing vitamins A and D from six months old. Some may need to begin from one month of age (see page 217).

Vitamin D is necessary for absorbing calcium and your baby needs a lot of vitamin D from six months when the stores they were born with will be running low. Breast milk is very low in vitamin D and babies may not make enough in their skin at this time, especially if it is winter or you keep their skin well covered. All breastfed babies are recommended to begin a vitamin D supplement from six months if they did not begin earlier.

Dark skinned babies of Asian, African, Afro-Caribbean and Middle Eastern origin are more likely to have very low vitamin D stores than white babies. This is due to a physiological difference between Caucasian babies (those with white skins) and babies of other races. The nature of the physiological difference is as yet unknown.

Babies who should have begun taking a vitamin D supplement from birth or one month of age are those who were likely to be born with low stores of vitamin D. Your baby will be likely to have had low vitamin D stores at birth if you had low stores of vitamin D yourself during the pregnancy. About one in four women have low stores of vitamin D. Mothers most likely to have low vitamin D stores are:

▶ *non-Caucasian mothers – that is those with dark pigmented skins*
▶ *those who spend little time outside, e.g. office and shop workers*
▶ *those who cover most of their skin when they are outside*
▶ *those living in northern areas of the UK where the sun's rays are weaker.*

Blood tests to check vitamin D levels are not done routinely on pregnant women so there is no way of knowing what your vitamin D stores were at the beginning of your pregnancy or during it.

Vitamin A is necessary for normal growth and development and many babies do not get enough from their food.

As a preventative measure, all breastfed babies should begin vitamin drops containing vitamin A and D from about six months old. Formula milks are fortified with both these vitamins so formula-fed babies do not need to begin vitamin drops until they are drinking less that 500 ml (17 fl oz) each day. NHS Healthy Start Children's vitamin drops are suitable and good value and your health visitor should be able to tell you where to get them. Pharmacies also sell a range of suitable vitamin drops, but they usually contain other nutrients in addition to vitamins A and D, which increases the cost.

Insight
The extra nutrients in vitamin drops in addition to vitamins A and D are not necessarily needed if your baby is eating well, but will do no harm. If you can find simple vitamin drops with just vitamins A and D that is all you need buy.

Looking after new teeth

Your baby's first tooth might appear any time from before birth until about one year old. However, most babies get their first teeth around six to nine months and as soon as they appear it is time to begin looking after them. Milk teeth can decay and cause pain. Milk teeth also help with speech development and ensure the jaw grows to the size necessary for the second set of permanent teeth. Clean the teeth twice a day with a soft toothbrush and a tiny smear of fluoride-containing toothpaste.

Sterilizing bottles for milk-feeds

You do not need to sterilize bowls, spoons or cups before using them for feeding your baby, but you should take care to make sure they are very well cleaned. However, you should continue to sterilize bottles and teats for milk-feeds until your baby is 12 months old. This is because it is very difficult to remove all the traces of milk from bottles and teats and even tiny traces of milk left in a bottle that have remained there from the last feed can cause a baby to become seriously ill.

Learning by watching others eating

Watching other people eat is an important part of learning to eat because babies all learn by copying. While you are feeding your baby try to have something to eat yourself. You could have a couple of finger foods that you have offered him or if you prefer you can prepare yourself a small snack that you can nibble on while feeding him.

If he is awake and alert at your mealtimes include him at your meal so that he can see you and others eating. However, at this age he still needs to be fed by you or someone else and it can be difficult to eat your own meal while feeding him. Many mothers manage it though.

By nine months your baby should be enjoying mashed foods with soft lumps and feeding himself with some finger foods. He should be having different foods at each meal and may be taking less milk now than he was when weaning first began.

Menu plans

FOR SIX TO SEVEN MONTHS

	Day 1	Day 2	Day 3
Breakfast	Baby rice with mashed pear and milk	Baby porridge with mashed banana and milk	Breakfast wheat biscuit (e.g. Weetabix) with mashed strawberries and milk
Midday meal	Puréed lamb with mashed potato and cauliflower Finger food: cooked cauliflower florets	Poached white fish with vegetables Finger food: cooked broccoli florets	Pork with apple, parsnip and swede Finger food: cooked parsnip sticks
Evening meal	Mashed mango and yogurt Finger food: mango slices	Mashed cooked apple and pear Finger food: ripe pear slices	Mashed peach and apricot Finger food: peach slices

	Day 1	Day 2	Day 3
Breakfast	Baby rice with mashed pear and milk	Baby porridge with mashed banana and milk	Scrambled egg with toast
Midday meal	Poached mackerel with vegetables Finger food: potato pieces Avocado and banana yogurt	Chicken with rice and leeks Finger food: cooked carrot sticks Egg custard and slices of ripe pear	Beef stew with potato Finger foods: cooked carrot sticks Rice pudding with fruit
Evening meal	Scrambled egg with toast Finger food: toast fingers Mashed raspberries	Poached fish with mashed potato Finger food: potato chips Mashed peaches and slices of ripe peach	Pasta with red pepper sauce Finger food: cooked pasta pieces Mashed banana and slices of ripe banana

Recipes for mashed food with lumps and soft finger foods

1 SOFT FINGER FOODS

Soft vegetable pieces
Serving these with a savoury dish and encouraging your baby to pick them up and feed himself will make him feel more involved with the food. He will be developing his dexterity at the same time.

Steaming is the best way to cook these as the fingers retain their shape and don't get soggy. Experiment with:

- ▶ *broccoli florets*
- ▶ *cauliflower florets*
- ▶ *courgettes*
- ▶ *French green beans*
- ▶ *small tender runner beans*
- ▶ *parsnip*
- ▶ *potato*
- ▶ *sweet potato.*

Peel the root vegetables and cut into fingers about 8 cm/3 in long. Cut runner beans and courgettes into sticks of about the same length. Break the broccoli and cauliflower into small florets. Steam or boil the vegetable sticks until tender but not soft – about ten minutes.

Roasted vegetable sticks
Use any of the following vegetables:

- ▶ *beetroot*
- ▶ *carrot*
- ▶ *celeriac*
- ▶ *courgette*
- ▶ *parsnip*
- ▶ *peppers – use red or yellow*
- ▶ *potato*
- ▶ *sweet potato.*

1 tbsp rapeseed or olive oil
½ tsp ground cumin – optional but adds a lovely flavour

Preheat the oven to 200°C/350°F/gas mark 4.
Peel the vegetables, except the peppers and courgettes, and cut into the size of thick potato chips.

Courgettes and peppers – wash them first. Cut the courgettes into sticks the size of thick potato chips. Deseed the peppers and cut them into strips about ½ cm/¼ in wide.

Stir the ground cumin into the oil. Brush some oil onto a baking sheet on an oven tray. Place the vegetable sticks onto the baking sheet and brush them all over with the remaining oil. Put into the oven and bake for 15–25 minutes until the vegetables are tender. Remove from the oven and place the vegetable sticks on a paper towel to cool and absorb any excess oil.

These are best if made just before serving. You will enjoy them as well and can eat some while feeding your baby.

Soft fruit sticks

Most fruits make good finger foods for beginning to learn to chew. By choosing ripe fruit you will be making sure they are sweet and slightly soft. Uncooked fruits contain more vitamins than cooked ones as a small proportion is always destroyed with cooking. There is no need to wait for teeth as babies' gums are just as good with soft foods. These fruits are the best to start with:

- *banana*
- *kiwi*
- *mango*
- *melon*
- *nectarine*
- *papaya*
- *peach*
- *pear.*

Peel the fruit and stone or core it. Cut the fruit into pieces about 4–5 cm/2 in long and just thick enough for your baby to grasp.

2 BREAKFASTS

Creamy first porridge

As oats contain more iron than rice, introducing porridge as an alternative breakfast will increase your baby's iron intake. This is a very quick recipe using the microwave. It does freeze but as it is so quick to make you might as well eat the rest yourself and make it freshly each time. You can also make it with water or with half milk, half water.

2 tbsp porridge oats
150 ml/¼ pint milk or formula milk

Put the oats and milk in a wide soup bowl. Microwave on full power, uncovered, for three minutes. Allow to stand for a couple of minutes to thicken. You can purée this and/or push it through a sieve to make it very smooth. However, the lumps are very fine and soft and your baby will soon learn to cope with them. Take out a portion and thin down, stirring well, with more milk or formula milk, if necessary.

If you don't have a microwave then stir the oats and milk together in a saucepan and simmer gently on the hob until a soft, thick mixture forms. This takes about five to seven minutes.

Makes one serving for baby and a small portion for you.

Porridge with mashed banana
Porridge, one portion from the recipe above
¼ banana, mashed or puréed

Make the porridge as in the recipe above. Mash the banana while the porridge stands to cool and thicken further. Mix the banana with a portion of porridge.

Scrambled egg with finger food
1 egg
1 tbsp milk
1 tsp butter

Beat the egg with the milk in a small bowl. Melt the butter over a gentle heat in a small frying pan and pour in the egg mixture. Continue cooking over the gentle heat, stirring until the egg is just cooked right through but still soft. If you overcook egg it will become dry, hard and rubbery. Remove from the heat, allow to cool and serve immediately.

Serve with soft finger food such as steamed vegetable sticks and crusts from lightly toasted bread.

3 SAVOURY COURSES

The recipes below contain several servings. The remaining servings can all be frozen to use on following days.

Chicken with rice and leeks

30 g/2 tbsp white basmati or long grain white rice
200 ml/7 fl oz water
½ chicken breast (70 g/3 oz), skinned and cut into small pieces
½ small leek (40 g/1½ oz), washed thoroughly and thinly sliced
1 small carrot (30 g/1 oz), peeled and diced
1 tsp thyme

Put the rice grains in a sieve and wash well with water. Drain. Put the rice in a small pan and add the water. Bring to the boil and cover with a tight-fitting lid. Simmer for five minutes. Lift the lid and add the chicken, leek, carrot and thyme. Replace the lid and continue cooking until the chicken is cooked right through and the rice and leeks are tender (about 20 minutes). Add a little more water if necessary. Purée the mixture. Add some cooled, boiled water if you want a thinner purée.

Makes 4–6 servings.

Beef stew

Beef needs long, slow cooking to be really soft and tender so that you can mash it with the vegetables rather than puréeing. Prepare this dish early in the day or the day before so there is plenty of time. Casseroling in this way with vegetables gives a sweetish taste. You can purée the meat the first time you try but it should be soft enough to mash with the vegetables.

½ tbsp flour
½ tsp paprika
2 tsp rapeseed oil

110 g/4 oz lean braising steak, diced
½ small onion, thinly sliced
75 ml/2½ fl oz water or vegetable stock
½ small carrot, peeled and sliced
1 medium potato, peeled and diced
½ stick celery, sliced
½ small parsnip, peeled and diced
6 small button mushrooms
½ tsp dried thyme

Preheat the oven to 150°C/300°F/gas mark 1. Mix the flour and
paprika together in a small bowl and toss the meat in this to coat with
flour. Heat the oil in a frying pan, add the onion and stir-fry for a
few minutes. Then add the floured meat. Keep stirring until the meat
is browned on the outside. This will only take two to three minutes.
Add the water or stock and stir for one minute to incorporate all
the flour and juices. Remove from the heat and transfer to a small
casserole dish. Add the vegetables and thyme then cover and cook in
the oven for between two and three hours. Purée or mash with a fork
and serve with some steamed carrots or sweet potato as finger food.

Makes 4–5 servings.

Pork with apple, parsnip and swede
Pork loin chops are a tender cut. Ask the butcher to cut the bone
and fat away for you, or do so yourself. Pork is a red meat and
provides a good source of iron, zinc and B vitamins.

Lean pork from a thin loin chop (about 60 g/2 oz), cut into small
cubes
½ dessert apple, peeled and cored
½ medium parsnip (about 50 g/2 oz), peeled and cut into thin slices
60 g/2 oz swede, peeled and diced
100 ml/3½ fl oz water

Dice the apple. Pour the water into a small saucepan and bring to
the boil. Add in the pork, apple and both vegetables. Cover with
a tight-fitting lid and simmer until meat is cooked right through

and the vegetables are soft – at least 15 minutes. Take out some of the parsnip sticks to offer as finger food and purée the rest with the remaining water. Take out one portion and add some cooled, boiled water if you would like a thinner purée.

For slow cooking put all the ingredients in a small casserole dish and bake in the oven at 180°C/350°F/gas mark 4 for 45 minutes to one hour. It will be ready when the meat flakes easily when pushed with a fork.

Makes 4–6 servings.

Poached white fish with vegetables
Now your baby is over six months you can introduce fish. Poached fish is soft and using milk gives it a creamy taste. This recipe works just as well for any white fish including cod and plaice fillets.

½ sweet potato (about 60 g/2 oz), peeled and diced
7–8 small broccoli florets (about 60 g/2 oz)
85 g/3 oz fresh haddock fillet, skinned and boned
100 ml/3½ fl oz milk
1 tsp fresh fennel leaves, chopped

Steam the sweet potato and broccoli florets or simmer gently for ten minutes in 75 ml/2½ fl oz boiling water. While the vegetables are cooking, pour the milk into a small non-stick pan. Place the haddock fillet in the milk and heat. Gently simmer, uncovered, until the haddock is well cooked and turns white right through (seven or eight minutes). Mash the haddock and remaining milk with a fork. Check carefully for any remaining bones and remove them. Take out two broccoli florets for finger foods and mash the fennel and the remaining broccoli and sweet potato into the mashed fish.

Makes 4–6 servings.

Mackerel with vegetables
Mackerel, which is an oily fish, is a very good source of omega 3 fats and has more iron than white fish. Fresh mackerel has a

delicate flavour unlike the smoked variety and is available from good fishmongers.

100 ml/3½ fl oz water
1 small potato, peeled and diced
4 cauliflower florets
3 tbsp frozen green beans
75 ml/2½ fl oz milk
85 g/3 oz fresh mackerel fillet, skinned and washed
1 tsp fresh dill or chives chopped finely

Put the water in a small pan and bring to the boil. Add the potato and put the cauliflower florets on top. Simmer for five minutes and then add the frozen beans. Simmer for a further five to eight minutes until the potatoes are soft and the beans are hot right through. Meanwhile, put the milk in a non-stick frying pan, bring to the boil and add the mackerel fillet. Simmer, uncovered, for seven or eight minutes until the mackerel is cooked right through. Flake the fish into the milk checking very carefully and removing any bones. Add the vegetables and herbs to the fish and mash together with a fork.

Makes 4–6 servings.

Pasta with tomato and pepper sauce
55 g/2 oz any short pasta shapes
2 tsp olive oil
1 red pepper, seeded and chopped
1 small courgette, chopped
4 tbsp chopped tomatoes, tinned
2 tsp fresh basil or thyme, chopped
1 tbsp cheddar cheese, grated

Cook the pasta shapes until soft, according to instructions on the packet. Drain. Heat the oil in a small frying pan and then add the pepper and cook for about five minutes to soften. Add the courgette, tinned tomatoes and herbs and simmer gently for 15 minutes. Blend to a smooth sauce with a hand blender. Keep aside three or four pasta shapes as finger foods and add the remainder to the tomato sauce. Add the grated cheese which should melt into the sauce. Mash with a fork to break the pasta into smaller pieces. Serve with cooked vegetable sticks.

Makes 2–4 servings.

4 *MILK PUDDINGS*

Egg custard
It is easy enough to make custard using custard powder and following the instructions on the tin. However, using an egg to thicken the custard makes a more nutritious milk pudding.

½ tsp caster sugar
1 egg
150 ml/¼ pint milk
½ tsp vanilla extract

Preheat oven to 150°C/300°F/gas mark 1. Beat the sugar and egg together until the sugar dissolves. Whisk in the hot milk and vanilla extract and pour into a small, ovenproof dish. Bake until set – about 30–45 minutes.

Makes 2–4 servings.

Avocado and banana yogurt
Both these fruits, when ripe, will purée beautifully and do not need to be cooked. Even a blender may not be necessary. Make the purée just before you use it as the fruit discolours on standing.

¼ ripe banana, peeled and sliced
¼ ripe avocado, peeled and stoned
3 tbsp full fat bio yogurt

Mash the fruit together with a fork. Stir into the yogurt.

Makes 1–2 servings.

Rice pudding with fruit

In a couple of minutes you can prepare a rice pudding to bake in the oven during the morning and you will have a rich creamy pudding ready to serve for lunch. Any puréed fruit can be used.

1 ½ tbsp pudding rice
280 ml/½ pint milk
3 tbsp puréed fruit

Preheat the oven to 150°C/300°F/gas mark 1. Wash the rice with cold water and drain. Put in an ovenproof bowl and pour on the milk. Bake in the oven for two hours. Stir the pudding two or three times in the first 25 minutes to mix in any skin that forms. This ensures a creamy pudding. Mix equal quantities of pudding with puréed fruit to serve.

Makes 2–4 servings.

END-OF-CHAPTER QUESTIONS

1   *Which foods should you continue to avoid beyond six months?*

2   *From what age should your baby move onto thicker purées and then mashed food with soft lumps?*

3   *When should you begin offering your baby soft finger foods?*

4   *What should you offer with meals once they have become more than just a few teaspoonfuls?*

5   *Which foods provide good sources of iron for six- to nine-month-old babies?*

6   *From about what age should you begin to offer two courses at each meal – one savoury and one dessert (e.g. yogurt and fruit).*

7   *What should you do if your baby spits out lumps in his food?*

8   *Why should you encourage your baby to play with his food and self-feed with finger foods?*

9   *What signals might your baby use to tell you he has had enough?*

10 *What makes a nutritious savoury course?*

11 *Do you need to sterilize bottles, teats and cups for milk?*

12 *When should babies begin on a vitamin supplement?*

Starting family foods and eating with the family (nine months to one year)

In this chapter you will learn:
- *how to cut down on milk-feeds*
- *how to change to minced and chopped food*
- *how to change from a bottle to a cup*
- *how to move on to family foods.*

By nine months your toddler should be enjoying three meals per day with four or five milk-feeds. He will have experienced different tastes and should be chewing soft lumps and feeding himself with soft finger foods. His food should be very thickly mashed food with soft lumps. He should have mastered drinking from a cup with a free-flow spout. The next three months will be the final phase of weaning as you should aim to have him eating all the family foods you will be feeding him as a toddler by the time he is around 12 months old.

Changes to make to the feeding pattern

DROPPING THE EARLY MORNING MILK-FEED

When your baby is around nine to ten months old you may find that he is not as desperately hungry when he wakes up. This is a good time to stop giving him the early morning feed and give him his breakfast earlier instead. This change is important because it will encourage him to eat more solid foods first thing in the morning when he is hungry after about 12 hours' sleep rather than relying on a large milk-feed to fill him up. Offer some high-iron foods for breakfast such as:

▶ *porridge or a breakfast cereal that has added iron*
▶ *egg with toast.*

Serve both with some fruit to aid the iron absorption. You will be both increasing his intake of iron and cutting down his milk intake at the same time. These are both key parts of weaning at this stage. Finish his breakfast with a milk-feed. If he is on formula milk offer it in a cup with a free-flow spout rather than a bottle.

Insight

I can remember this happening quite naturally with my son. One morning he didn't seem desperate for a feed so I changed him and took him downstairs and popped him into his highchair. It meant an early breakfast for both of us for a while but with time he was happy to wait a bit longer for breakfast and have it with the rest of the family.

MOVING ON TO MINCED AND CHOPPED FOODS

During these three months you need to change gradually from offering mashed foods to offering minced and chopped foods. As you change the texture to harder foods he will learn to manage these by chewing more which is good for his jaw development.

He will only learn how to eat harder textures if you give him the opportunity to try. At first he may cough back lumps of harder textured food but this is part of him learning to cope with these textures. As long as he is sitting upright with good head control when he tries these foods it should not be a problem. He will cough back the lump, re-chew it and try swallowing it again.

Always stay close by in case of actual choking. If this occurs try not to panic and scare your baby. Just turn him upside down and gently pat him on the back. The lump should come back into the mouth by virtue of gravity. Cuddle your child and reassure him that nothing is wrong. You do not want to dramatize the occurrence so that he becomes scared of eating foods.

Figure 4.1 If your baby is choking, turn him upside down and pat his back.

Cut up hard foods into bite-size pieces, otherwise he may break off a piece that is too large for him to manage in his mouth.

▶ Fruit – *cut it rather than mashing it and you can now give harder pieces of raw fruit as finger foods, e.g. ripe apples and pears.*
▶ Vegetables – *when you have cooked vegetables just cut them up rather than mashing them. You can offer more raw vegetables such as sticks of cucumber and later sticks of raw carrot.*
▶ Meat – *use minced meat or slow-cooked tender cuts of meat which can be cut up rather than mashed, e.g. casseroles or stews; slow-roasted or gently stir-fried chicken; and minced meat in shepherds pie or cottage pie.*
▶ *All* cooked fish *has a soft texture and is suitable.*
▶ Bread *can be offered in small sandwiches as he should be able to bite and chew sandwiches with soft fillings.*

INTRODUCING HARDER FINGER FOODS

You can now offer harder finger foods, such as those listed below.

Harder finger foods

Pieces of raw fruit, e.g. apple, pear
Fruits with the pips or stones removed, e.g. cherries, grapes and
   segments of oranges, satsumas and clementines
Raw vegetables, e.g. sticks of cucumber, carrot, pepper,
   courgette
Breadsticks and crackers
Toast fingers
Pitta bread strips with humous
Rice cakes
Sandwiches with soft fillings
Slices of hard boiled egg
Mini sausages

INCREASING THE VARIETY OF FOODS OFFERED

As well as offering harder textures also offer different flavours by
offering different foods. A good guide is to think about the foods
you will offer your baby as a toddler. Try to offer all these foods
by the time he is around 12 months old. This will be easier if this
is your second or third baby because you can start feeding your
baby with your older children. However, if your baby is your first
then try to think ahead. If your own diet is not that which you
wish your toddler to eat then think about changing to a more
nutritious diet for the whole family. You will all then be able to
eat together.

When you are preparing his meals start adding the spices and herbs
you use in cooking so that he learns to like these flavours.

If you have used commercial baby foods up until now, change over
to at least some of the foods you eat. You can offer them alongside
commercial baby foods but it is particularly important that your

baby learns now to like the foods you want him to eat in the next couple of years. During his second year he will become more resistant to accepting new foods, so it is best to begin offering them now.

OFFERING TWO NUTRITIOUS COURSES AT ALL MEALTIMES

Babies can become bored with one course of food but still be hungry and interested to try another course. Offer two courses at each meal. Begin with a savoury course of:

- ▶ *meat, fish, eggs or pulses*
- ▶ *and a starchy food*
- ▶ *and vegetables.*

Then offer a second course or pudding which will be based on fruit and/or milk. As long as you make the second course a nutritious one you do not have to feel guilty about offering it. A pudding is nutritious if it contains one or more of the following ingredients:

- ▶ *fruit*
- ▶ *milk*
- ▶ *eggs*
- ▶ *flour*
- ▶ *rice or other cereals such as sago or tapioca*
- ▶ *finely ground or chopped nuts*
- ▶ *cocoa.*

All these ingredients provide your baby with nutrients. If there is a little added sugar to make the dish enjoyable then this doesn't matter.

Avoid seeing the second course as a reward
Do not fall into the trap of seeing the second course as a reward for having eaten the first course – even if you learned this as a child yourself. You will be teaching your baby that the pudding is

a more desirable food than the savoury course. This is of course the opposite to the health message you would wish him to learn. Be confident that the pudding has many nutrients in it and give it to your baby even if he has eaten very little of the savoury course.

Insight

Babies naturally prefer sweet food so will usually eat this course well. Just limit it to a small portion.

Encouraging self-feeding skills

Your baby will still not be able to feed himself quickly enough to satisfy his hunger so you need to continue feeding him. However, it is important that he feels involved in the feeding process so give him finger foods at each meal and his own spoon so that he can copy what you are doing with a spoon. He may try to feed you as you feed him. Continue to let him play with the food by putting his fingers into bowls of soft food. It is important he uses all his senses, including touch, to become familiar with foods and learn all about them.

Figure 4.2 Make sure your baby feels involved in the feeding process.

Finishing meals with smaller milk-feeds

As your baby eats more solids he will cut back on his milk-feeds himself. Offer a little less milk and respect his decision when he has had enough. He may drink more after some meals than others depending on how much he has eaten.

CUTTING OUT ANOTHER MILK-FEED

If your baby is eating a large milk pudding at one meal you can stop offering him his usual milk-feed at the end of that meal. By 11–12 months he should only be having two or three milk-feeds each day:

- ▶ *one after breakfast or mid morning*
- ▶ *one before bed*
- ▶ *one other smaller feed after one of his other meals or in between meals.*

Insight

Giving milk after breakfast, not before on waking, is key to getting your baby to eat a good breakfast.

USING CUPS RATHER THAN BOTTLES

During these three months try to change from giving the milk-feeds from bottles to giving them from cups. It is best to make this change by 12 months as babies older than this begin to associate feeding from a bottle with comfort and they can quite stubbornly refuse to change to a cup. It takes longer to drink a feed from a bottle and teat than from a free-flow, spouted cup and the milk sugar lactose will be in contact with his teeth for a longer time. The more time teeth are bathed in sweet liquids the more likely they are to decay. This is especially important at night when there is less saliva in the mouth. Saliva helps to protect the teeth from decay.

Insight

Changing to cups can be a damp affair if there are spills.
You can always help your baby not to spill by supporting the
cup while he takes the lead with his hands on the handles.

Learning to drink by himself

Continue to offer your baby a cup of water with his meals and
encourage him to hold the cup to begin to learn how to drink by
himself. He will also be willing to hold his bottle as well if you are
using one for milk-feeds. Allow him to do this when he is sitting up
and alert. Do not give him a drink in either a cup or a bottle and
leave him alone with it, such as putting him to bed with a bottle of
milk or any other drink. It is unsafe as he may choke on the liquid.
At bedtime give him his milk-feed in a cup or bottle while he is still
awake and put him into bed when he has finished the drink.

Insight

The bottle of milk just before bedtime is such a part of the
bedtime routine that this is the bottle most parents give up
last. Once your baby is adept with the cup he will accept this
change quite easily around 12 months. The longer you leave
it the more difficult it is to change, especially with stubborn
babies who do not like change.

Vitamin supplements

Breastfed babies should have begun vitamin supplements at around
six months. Formula milk contains vitamins A and D, and while
your baby is still drinking at least 500 ml/17 fl oz of formula each
day he will be getting enough of these vitamins from his formula
milk. However, as he eats more food and reduces his formula
intake to less than 500 ml/17 fl oz you need to begin giving him a
vitamin supplement containing vitamins A and D each day.

Figure 4.3 Encourage your baby to learn to drink by himself.

Insight

Parents are surprised that babies who eat well should have supplements, but most vitamin D is made in the skin and little comes from food. As we keep babies well covered in clothing and mostly indoors nowadays, it is a vitamin they rarely get enough of it. Vitamin A is the vitamin babies are least likely to eat enough of. It is very important for their immunity.

Developing a positive attitude to food and meals

EATING TOGETHER AS A FAMILY

Include your baby in as many family meals as you can. He will be learning how to eat by watching you. He will also be happy to try the foods that you are eating. In fact, he will be keen to try food off your plate and you should allow him to do this.

MAKING MEALS SOCIABLE AND ENJOYABLE OCCASIONS

Keep meals as fun, enjoyable occasions. Remember to allow your baby to decide the quantity he will eat. Praise him for eating some when he has finished eating and you are taking the plate away, even if he has not eaten all of it. Do not coerce him into eating more when he has indicated he has had enough. Respect your baby's decision that he has had enough as his appetite will vary from day to day.

Insight

Smiling and remaining calm when your baby rejects your lovingly prepared food is really hard. I remember that painful disappointment even now – many years on. There is no easy way, particularly for the control freaks among us. Just remember, he has a right to decide whether he eats or not – no matter who has prepared the food.

Figure 4.4 Include your baby in as many family meals as you can.

EATING WITHOUT DISTRACTIONS

Babies can really only concentrate on one activity at a time, so do not have distractions around while he is eating. Do not have the TV on or include toys or games during mealtime. Instead, talk to your baby about the food he is eating and say positive things about the food.

By about 12 months, your baby will have ideas about what foods he likes and what those foods look like. Your baby should:

▶ *recognize foods by sight*
▶ *know whether he likes the taste or not*
▶ *be able to sense most food textures.*

Those babies who have not been offered a wide variety of tastes and textures by 12 months are more likely to be fussy eaters.

Insight

Many mothers slip food into their baby's mouth while he is watching TV, for the satisfaction of feeling that he has eaten more. However, this is not a step forwards because he is not learning about the taste and appearance of food while you are slipping it in. At this stage that is actually more important than how much he eats.

Is he getting enough?

The amount your baby eats or drinks at this age might be quite different to another baby of the same age. If your baby seems happy and content then he is getting enough. Growth rates slow down from around six months and breastfed babies often grow more slowly than formula-fed babies around this age. Slower weight gain at this age is more desirable than rapid weight gain. Babies who gain weight rapidly at this age are more likely to go on to become overweight as children. If your baby is contented with his meals and feeds then there is no need to encourage him to eat more.

Some mothers find it upsetting when their baby does not eat all the food they have been offered, especially if it has been lovingly prepared from fresh ingredients. However, it is important to allow babies to develop a sense of when they have eaten enough and to have that decision respected. They are able to self-regulate their intake of calories to match their energy needs fairly accurately.

It is important that you allow them to do this by respecting their decision when they indicate they have had enough.

Using commercial baby foods for convenience

You may be out and about with your baby more now and using commercial foods may be more convenient. Choose those with a similar texture to that which you have already been offering him. This may not correspond exactly to his age as textures in baby foods tend to be smoother than babies are able to manage.

Unfortunately, if you have rarely used commercial foods, when you offer one while you are travelling or away from home he may be unwilling to eat much of it because it will be a new taste. If he refuses most of this meal do not despair – one meal refused will not matter. If he eats very little at one meal he can make up for this by eating more at the next meal.

Alternatively, there may be food available that you can just cut up small or mash for your baby. Just check that there isn't a lot of salt added in the cooking. He may surprise you by enjoying something you haven't offered before.

Insight

I only used commercial baby foods when we were travelling and they were always refused because the taste is quite different from home-prepared foods. In the end I stopped bothering and just offered a bit of whatever was going in the restaurant or café. I remember my daughter once eating plain boiled rice rather than a jar of baby food.

Feeding routine

Your baby will be spending more time awake now and may be crawling about and playing with toys. Try to keep to a routine of meals around your baby's sleeping pattern so that you are not attempting to feed him just before a meal when he is tired.

> **Insight**
>
> I used to make the mistake of offering a meal just before a daytime sleep, and found it very frustrating until I changed the routine and gave a quick snack before the sleep and then the meal when he woke up.

Your routine may be like this:

Early morning:	Wakes – no milk-feed
Breakfast:	Cereal and milk and fruit or egg and toast with fruit juice. Finish with a milk-feed from a cup – he may prefer this later before he goes down for his sleep.
Sleep during the morning	
Lunch:	Two courses with finger foods – one savoury, one based on milk. Water to drink with the meal, no milk-feed.
Sleep during the afternoon	
Tea:	Two courses with finger foods. Water in a cup with the meal. Finish with a small milk-feed in a cup.

Bedtime routine

Milk-feed in a cup or bottle before going into bed.

Your baby may become thirsty between meals – especially in hot weather or if he has a cold with a runny nose. If he cries, offer him some water in a cup to see if he is thirsty.

Menu plans

Time	Course	Day 1	Day 2	Day 3
Breakfast		Porridge with mashed fruit	Baby muesli with milk	Boiled egg with toast
	Finger foods	Banana slices	Blueberries	Kiwi fruit slices
		Milk-feed	Milk-feed	Milk-feed
Midday meal	First course	Chicken and vegetable stir-fry with rice	Fried fish fillet with mashed sweet potato and peas	Lamb casserole with green beans
	Finger foods	Broccoli florets	Steamed sweet potato sticks	Green beans
	Second course	Banana with custard	Rice pudding with fruit and cinnamon	Yogurt and mashed peach
	Finger foods	Banana slices	Pear slices	Ripe peach slices
	Drinks	Water	Water	Water

(Contd)

Time	Course	Day 1	Day 2	Day 3
Evening meal	First course	Scrambled egg with toast	Macaroni cheese	Humous sandwiches
	Finger foods	Toast fingers	Cooked macaroni pieces	Carrot and cucumber sticks
	Second course	Apple and pear compote	Yogurt and mashed raspberries	Strawberries and fromage frais
	Finger foods	Apple slices	Raspberries and grapes	Fresh strawberries
	Drinks	Water and milk-feed to finish	Water and milk-feed to finish	Water and milk-feed to finish

Family food recipes

1 HARDER FINGER FOODS

Fruit finger foods
Preparation of the fruits varies:

Cherries	Wash and remove the stones.
Grapes	Wash, cut in half and remove any pips.
Strawberries	Wash, remove the green stalk, cut large strawberries in half.
Raspberries	Wash and remove inner stalk.

Apples	Peel and cut into segments. Offer them washed and unpeeled as he gets older.
Pears	
Peaches	
Apricots	

Clementines	Peel and break into segments. Carefully remove all pips. Large segments may need to be cut in half.
Oranges	
Satsumas	
Tangerines	

Raw vegetable sticks
Preparation varies:

Carrots, cucumbers, courgettes	Peel and cut into thin sticks or thin slices.
Peppers	Wash, cut open and remove the stalk and inner seeds. Cut the remainder into thin sticks.
Tomatoes	Wash and cut into small segments.
Celery	Wash and cut into thin sticks or thin slices.

Paprika potato wedges
1 tbsp olive oil
1 cloves garlic, crushed (optional)
¼ tsp paprika
½ tsp oregano
1 large potato, cut into thick wedges
Preheat the oven to 220°C/450°F/gas mark 7. Mix the oil, crushed garlic, paprika, and oregano together in a bowl. Add the potato wedges and toss them in the oil mixture. Place on a hot baking tray and cook in oven for 40–45 minutes until crisp. Turn by loosening with a spatula after about 30 minutes.

Makes 2–4 servings.

2 BREAKFAST

Porridge with mashed fruit
The soft lumps of both porridge and cooked fruit will be easy for your baby to manage. As an alternative to apple, use ripe pear, peach, apricot or plum depending on the season.

2 tbsp porridge oats
$\frac{1}{4}$–$\frac{1}{2}$ small dessert apple, peeled, cored and finely diced
150 ml/$\frac{1}{4}$ pint water/milk

Put oats, apple and water or milk in a wide soup bowl. Microwave on full power, uncovered, for three minutes. Allow the porridge to stand for a few minutes to cool and thicken. Stir with a fork and use this to mash the pieces of fruit. Serve with extra milk or formula milk.

Baby muesli
1 tbsp rolled oats
1 tbsp sultanas
$\frac{1}{2}$ tbsp dried apricots, finely chopped
1 tbsp wheatgerm
1 tbsp ground almonds
3 tbsp unsweetened apple, orange or pineapple juice

Mix the oats, sultanas and dried apricots together. Process them in a food processor for about 30 seconds to make sure they are finely chopped. Transfer to a serving bowl and add in the wheatgerm and ground almonds. Pour in the fruit juice and leave to soak for a few minutes to soften. Serve with milk or yogurt.

Makes 1–2 servings.

3 SOFT COOKED SAVOURY DISHES

Be sure to wash all vegatables throughly before use.

Chicken and vegetable stir-fry
Stir-fried chicken breast will remain soft enough for infants to chew. Other meats cooked this way may be too tough.

1 tbsp olive oil
½ a chicken breast, thinly sliced
½ tsp dried tarragon
½ red pepper, deseeded and thinly sliced
1 small courgette, thinly sliced
6 small broccoli florets

Heat the oil in a non-stick frying pan. Add the chicken slices
and tarragon and stir-fry for a few minutes. Add the red pepper,
courgette and broccoli florets and continue stir-frying over a
gentle heat until the chicken has cooked right through (about
15 minutes). Serve with rice, pasta or steamed potatoes. Cut the
chicken into small pieces.

Makes 2–4 servings.

Roast chicken
By slowly roasting a chicken you will find the meat is soft and can
be mashed or cut into small manageable pieces.

1 small chicken
½ onion, peeled and cut in half
½ lemon
Small handful of fresh herbs or 2 tsp dried herbs

Preheat the oven to 190°C/375°F/gas mark 5. Rinse the chicken
with water both inside the cavity and on the outside. Place in
a roasting tin. Put the onion, lemon and fresh herbs into the
cavity of the chicken. Put in the oven and cook for about one
hour. This will vary depending on the size of the chicken but
allow about 25 minutes for every 450 g/1 lb plus an additional
25 minutes. The chicken is cooked when all the juices run clear
and the leg can easily be tugged away from the body. When
cooked, remove from the oven and allow to rest for ten minutes
before carving.

Lamb casserole
Lamb is another meat that becomes very tender when cooked
slowly in a casserole.

1 lamb cutlet, cut into small cubes
2 spring onions, thinly sliced
1 medium potato, cut in half
¼ small aubergine, diced
¼ red pepper, deseeded and thinly sliced
1 tomato, diced
100 ml/3½ fl oz water
½ tsp dried rosemary

Preheat the oven to 180°C/350°F/gas mark 4. Place all the ingredients in a small casserole dish. Cook in the oven for 10–15 minutes until bubbling then turn the temperature down to 150°C/300°F/gas mark 2. Continue to cook for a further 45 minutes until the lamb is very tender when it will break apart with the push of a fork. Remove from the oven and mash the potatoes and vegetables into the juices, at the same time breaking up the pieces of lamb.

Makes 1–2 servings.

Moroccan lamb with couscous
A very mildly spiced lamb dish to introduce more tastes to your baby's palate.

1 tsp ground cumin
1 tsp ground coriander
¼ tsp nutmeg
110 g/4 oz lean lamb neck fillet, trimmed and diced
1 tbsp olive oil
2 tbsp diced aubergine
1 tsp grated fresh ginger or ½ tsp ground ginger
½ clove garlic, crushed
½ can chopped tomatoes (200 g/7 oz)
6 tbsp/80 g couscous grains
200 ml/7 fl oz boiling water

Mix the ground spices together in a bowl. Toss the cubes of lamb into the mixed spices and stir well until the lamb is well coated. Heat the oil in a frying pan and fry the lamb until browned.

Add the diced aubergine and continue frying, stirring for two minutes. Add in the ginger and garlic and fry for another minute. Add the chopped tomatoes, cover tightly with a lid and simmer gently for about one hour, until the lamb is tender when it will break apart when pushed with a fork. Put the couscous in a bowl and pour over the boiling water. Leave to stand or five minutes so that the water is all absorbed. Fluff up the couscous with a fork and stir into the lamb dish. Take out one portion and cut the lamb into small bite-size pieces.

Makes 4–6 servings.

Shepherd's pie
A family favourite which is traditionally made with minced lamb but you can use minced beef instead.

½ tbsp olive oil
1 small onion, peeled and finely chopped
1 tbsp chopped thyme
1 tbsp chopped rosemary
220 g/½ lb minced lean lamb
1 small carrot, finely diced
1 clove garlic, peeled and crushed
½ tbsp flour
½ tbsp tomato purée
150 ml/¼ pint water
200g/½ lb potatoes, peeled and cut into chunks
½ tbsp butter
50 ml/2 fl oz milk

Heat the olive oil in a pan and add the onion and herbs. Cook over a gentle heat until soft. Add the minced lamb, garlic and carrot and continue cooking until the lamb is brown right through. Add the flour, and tomato purée and stir well. Cook for one minute, then gradually add the water, bring to the boil, cover and simmer for 20 minutes. Meanwhile, steam the potatoes or boil in a small amount of water. Mash the potatoes with the butter and milk.

Preheat the oven to 200°C/400°F/gas mark 6. Put the meat mixture into an ovenproof dish and cover with the mashed potatoes. Bake for 30 minutes or until lightly browned on top. Serve with some roasted vegetables which can cook in the oven at the same time as the pie.

Makes 6–8 servings.

Fried fish fillet
Fish cooks quickly so it really is fast food. Whether grilled or fried it takes just a few minutes to cook. It then flakes very easily and will go with any combination of rice, pasta or potatoes and can be accompanied with vegetables.

1 fillet of fresh, white fish, skinned and deboned
juice of 1 lemon
1 tbsp olive oil or butter

Melt the oil or butter in a non-stick frying pan. Drizzle half the lemon juice over one side of the fish and put into the pan with the lemony side down. Drizzle the rest of the lemon onto the upturned side. Allow to cook over a very gentle heat for about two or three minutes and then turn over and cook the other side. The fish is cooked when it has changed colour all the way through. Flake the fish with a fork, checking carefully for any remaining bones. Serve with rice, pasta or mashed potato and one or two vegetables.

Makes 4–8 servings.

Macaroni cheese
This traditional pasta dish often becomes a favourite of many babies and toddlers.

40 g/1½ oz macaroni or any other short pasta
15 g/½ oz butter
1 tbsp flour
150 ml/¼ pint milk
40 g/1½ oz cheddar cheese, grated
pinch paprika

Cook the macaroni or pasta until soft, according to instructions on the packet. Drain. Melt the butter in a saucepan and then add in the flour. Cook for about two minutes on a low heat – the flour should not turn brown. Pour the milk in slowly while stirring with a wooden spoon or balloon whisk. Keep stirring until you have a smooth sauce. Bring to the boil and simmer gently for two or three minutes until the sauce thickens. Remove from the heat and stir in the grated cheese, paprika and cooked macaroni or pasta. Mash with a fork to break the macaroni into small pieces if necessary. Serve with cooked vegetable sticks.

Makes 2–4 servings.

4 NUTRITIOUS PUDDINGS

Rice pudding with cinnamon and fruit

By adding fruit and cinnamon to this traditional children's dessert your child will be experiencing a wider range of flavours at a critical time. Use other seasonal fruit if sweet English apples are not available.

40 g/1½ oz pudding rice
1 tsp sugar
1 dessert apple, peeled, cored and sliced
2 tbsp sultanas
375 ml/13 fl oz milk
½ tsp ground cinnamon

Preheat the oven to 150°C/300°F/gas mark 2. Rinse the rice and drain well. Place all the ingredients in a shallow ovenproof dish and stir well. Place in the oven and bake for 1½ –2 hours or until the rice is soft. It is also delicious cold.

Makes 2–4 servings.

Banana with custard
280 ml/½ pint milk
1 tbsp custard powder
½ banana, sliced

Put the custard powder in a bowl and add 3 tbsp milk and stir to dissolve the custard powder. Put the remainder of the milk in a small saucepan and bring to the boil. Pour the boiling milk into the bowl with the custard powder and stir to mix the powder through. Pour the contents of the bowl back into the saucepan and put back onto the heat. Stir continuously until the custard thickens. Put the banana slices into a small serving bowl and pour on half the custard. Make sure the custard has cooled sufficiently before feeding your baby.

Makes 2 servings of custard.

END-OF-CHAPTER QUESTIONS

1 *When should you stop the early morning milk-feed?*

2 *From what age should you begin offering minced and chopped foods and hard finger foods?*

3 *What are hard finger foods?*

4 *At what age should you discontinue offering milk in bottles?*

5 *What should reduce as your baby begins to eat more?*

6 *When should you begin giving your baby a vitamin supplement with vitamins A and D?*

7 *Why should you include babies at as many family meals as possible?*

5

Feeding preterm babies

In this chapter you will learn:
- *how preterm babies are fed before they can suck from a breast/bottle*
- *about choices of milk for preterm babies*
- *when to wean*
- *how to minimize the chance of later feeding problems.*

What is a preterm baby?

Babies who are born before spending 37 weeks or more in the womb are known as preterm babies.

A normal pregnancy lasts 40 weeks but doctors will allow a pregnancy to go on until 42 weeks before they induce the birth of a baby. Any babies born between 37 and 42 weeks are known as term babies.

Your baby's gestational age at birth is the time your baby has spent in your womb. A baby born after 29 weeks growing inside you will be known by medical staff as born at 29 weeks' gestation. He will be considered to have been born 11 weeks (40 – 29 = 11) early.

Preterm babies are born early for a variety of reasons but often it is because there is a medical problem. Babies can survive now when born as young as about 23 weeks' gestation.

The needs and care of preterm babies will vary according to their gestational age when they were born and whether they have any particular medical problems.

Feeding in hospital

Babies born very young are not able to feed well enough to get enough nutrients by sucking from a breast or bottle. Depending on their gestational age at birth and their medical condition, they will be fed by any combination of the following methods.

▶ *Intravenous feeding (IV feeding) or parenteral nutrition. This involves giving a special liquid via a very fine tube into one of the baby's veins. The nutrients he needs are going straight into the blood. At first the liquid feed will be a mixture of sugar (glucose), salts and water. Later some amino acids (the building blocks of protein) plus some fats and vitamins and minerals may be added. IV feeding is used when a baby is too premature, too small or too unwell to digest milk.*

▶ *Trophic feeding usually happens in combination with IV feeding. As early as possible after birth a tiny tube will be threaded through the baby's nose or mouth and down into his stomach. Tiny amounts of milk will be slowly dripped in. These tiny amounts of milk will not be enough to feed the baby adequately on their own but will protect him from some diseases in the intestine such as necrotizing enterocolitis which is often called NEC.*

▶ *Tube-feeding involves milk being put into the baby's stomach via the same very fine tube. It is know as nasogastric feeding if the tube goes via his nose or orogastric feeding if the tube goes via his mouth. Small feeds are measured into a syringe and the feed is then connected to the feeding tube and allowed to drip slowly into the baby's stomach.*
Some babies may need transpyloric feeding when the tube is passed through the stomach and down into the small intestine. Small amounts of milk are fed continuously.

> *Tube-feeding is used when a baby's digestive system is ready for feeds by mouth but he cannot yet suckle and drink properly.*

▶ *Breast or bottle-feeding. Once a baby is able to manage sucking, swallowing and breathing all at the same time he can begin breast or bottle-feeding. Bottles will be very small ones only holding about 25–50 ml/1–2 fl oz of breast milk or a special formula milk. A special teat that is very small and flexible will be used.*

How much extra care with feeding will he need?

In the first few days after birth your baby will lose some weight as all babies do following their birth. This is quite normal as some of the loss is fluid and salts. The type of feeding he begins on will depend on:

▶ *his gestational age at birth*
▶ *the medical problems he may have had.*

If your baby was born at:

24–28 weeks' gestation he won't be able to feed for himself. He will probably be able to suck but he won't be able to co-ordinate the sucking, swallowing and breathing. This means he can't yet drink from your breast or a bottle without choking on the milk.

He will need to be fed intravenously at first with some trophic feeding beginning as soon as possible. With time, and as he is able to tolerate more milk via his tube, the intravenous feeding will be decreased.

29–34 weeks' gestation he may be able to suck strongly on your finger but he is unlikely to be able to breast- or bottle-feed. Until around 34 weeks' gestation, premature babies find it difficult to co-ordinate sucking, swallowing and breathing in the right order. Taking milk by mouth may still make him choke so he will need to be fed by tube. If you express a few drops of milk and leave them on your nipple he may be able to lick these off like a kitten. Some babies begin to cup feed at this time.

35–7 weeks' gestation (or 3–5 weeks early) he should be able to breast- or bottle-feed but may need some temporary help in the form of tube-feeding as he may not be strong enough to breast- or bottle-feed all the milk he needs.

Premature babies have tiny stomachs and can only take small feeds at a time. They need to be fed every two to four hours.

Milks used in tube-feeding

YOUR OWN EXPRESSED BREAST MILK

This is the best option for your baby as it:

▶ *is easier for him to digest and is absorbed more easily than formula milk*
▶ *will help his progress because of the growth factors and hormones that it contains*
▶ *will provide him with antibodies to protect him against diseases to which preterm babies are especially vulnerable. These antibodies are usually transferred via the placenta during the last three months of pregnancy. Premature babies will not have received these because of their early birth so providing them through your breast milk is the next best option.*

You are the only person who can do this for your baby and it may help you feel a very valuable part of the team looking after your baby.

You will need to express your breast milk and there are three ways of expressing: using electric pumps, hand pumps and hand expressing (see page 9). Not all mothers find expressing milk easy but staff on the baby care unit can help you with tips and support. Even if you only express a little bit this can be very valuable for your baby and he can have the rest of his milk requirement made up with banked expressed milk or formula milk.

> **Insight**
>
> Mothers of preterm babies have often had a traumatic time, with an unexpectedly early birth followed by adjusting to their baby needing complicated medical care. Expressing breast milk on top of all this may seem like another mountain to climb. There is usually a lot of help available to support you, but sometimes you need to ask for that support, because in a busy and short-staffed neonatal unit staff may forget to offer you the help and support that is available.

BANKED BREAST MILK

This is breast milk that has been donated to the hospital by other new mothers. Every step is taken to ensure this breast milk from another mother is safe for your baby. It will be pasteurized which means it is heated to destroy any viruses or bacteria. However, in this process the antibodies that boost the immunity of babies are lost, but it is still better for very young babies than formula milks.

BREAST MILK FORTIFIERS

This is a powder that is sometimes added to breast milk for premature babies. It adds some extra protein, minerals and vitamins to help your baby grow more quickly and prevent nutritional deficiencies.

SPECIAL FORMULA MILK FOR PREMATURE BABIES

These are special milks which are formulated for preterm babies with a different balance of nutrients to those found in normal formula milks. They have higher levels of protein and certain nutrients than formula milks for term babies. Three companies in the UK make preterm formula milks and they are all fairly similar. Your hospital will usually have a contract with one of the three manufacturers and will normally only provide one of them. The formulas used in hospitals are:

Cow & Gate Nutriprem 1
Aptamil Preterm
SMA Gold Prem 1

Insight
These preterm milks are made to the same nutritional content, so no one brand is better than another.

Beginning breastfeeding or bottle-feeding your baby

How soon your baby begins to breastfeed from you will depend on several factors including how early he was born and his medical condition. You can usually begin trying when he is about 35 weeks' gestation. However, he may continue to need some extra milk from the tube for a while.

You can begin trying to breastfeed while he still has a tube through his mouth or nose. Hold him so that the tube is on the side away from your breast so that he is still able to breathe. If the tube is through his mouth make sure it is taped at the side of his mouth and cheek rather than down over his bottom lip and chin.

Once he is successfully feeding entirely on milk you will be able to plan to take him home. He should be feeding every three or four hours and you may be able to keep this up at home. You will need to continue night-feeding as he will still need milk during the night. If you are using a formula milk you will need to change to a post-discharge formula such as:

Cow & Gate Nutriprem 2
SMA Gold Prem 2

When to wean preterm babies

Each preterm baby needs to be considered individually when it comes to deciding when to begin weaning. Because they were not in the womb during the last few weeks of pregnancy they have not built up the stores of certain nutrients that term babies will have done. Milk alone will not be enough for premature babies until about six months after their estimated date of delivery (EDD) and most premature babies will have vitamin and mineral supplements prescribed for them for this reason.

Because preterm babies have begun to use their intestines early in life, their digestive systems will be more developed. Experts recommend beginning weaning sometime between five and eight months after their actual birth date. The signs to look out for are:

▶ *He is watching with interest when other people are eating.*
▶ *He is putting things into his mouth.*
▶ *He seems ready for something new.*
▶ *He seems less satisfied with milk alone.*

It is best to discuss when to start weaning with your baby's healthcare team.

Preterm babies may not have good head control at this age so will need to have their back and head supported well so that there is no risk of choking. If you hold your baby you need to support his back and neck with your arm. A car seat or baby bouncer may be easier and you can use a small soft towel to give extra support for the neck in order to keep his head in a good position.

Begin with puréed foods as described in Chapter 2 and when he is managing spoon-feeding well, gradually thicken the purées and move on to mashed food. Do not delay the move to thicker mashes as he needs to learn to manage these and he will only do this as you give him the opportunity to learn.

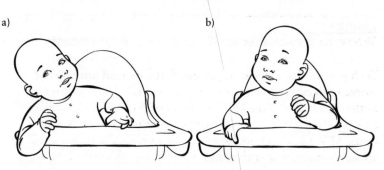

a)   b)

Figure 5.1 a) The position to avoid and b) the position to aim for when weaning your baby.

Insight

Parents of preterm babies are usually, understandably, more anxious about feeding and weaning their baby. However scared you are of your baby choking, you do need to progress from purées onto thicker mashes and soft lumps as soon as your baby is confidently managing food from a spoon. Staying on very smooth purée food for too long is not giving your baby the opportunity to learn to eat new textures.

Assessing the growth of your preterm baby

When your baby is weighed and measured, the healthcare professional will plot his measurements on the normal growth charts. Until he is one or two years old he should always be plotted using his corrected age rather than his actual age from the date of his birth. His corrected age is calculated by subtracting the number of weeks he was born early from his age since birth. For example if he was born at 29 weeks' gestation then he was born 11 weeks early (40 – 29 = 11). His corrected age will be 11 weeks or two and a half months less than his actual age. When he is nine months old and he is plotted on a growth chart as if he were a baby of nine months that was not born early he might appear on the growth chart as being very small. However, if he is plotted as only being six and a half months old (9 – 2½ months = 6½) then he should have a normal weight and length for that age.

Giving extra supplements

During the last few weeks in the womb, term babies lay down stores of most nutrients to last them through the first few months of life. As preterm babies were not in the womb during this time they will not have laid down these stores. For this reason they need extra vitamins and minerals. Doctors will normally prescribe suitable supplements. They will usually contain extra iron and vitamins A and D.

Feeding problems

Preterm babies are much more likely to get feeding problems as toddlers. The reasons for this may be linked to the many unpleasant and maybe even painful sensations around their mouth in their early weeks of life. These will have included:

▶ *large tubes for breathing inserted into their mouth*
▶ *nasal and oral feeding tubes taped and re-taped to their cheeks*
▶ *unpleasant medicines syringed into their mouth.*

Another reason may be that mothers of premature babies are particularly anxious about all aspects of their care and are often more anxious around feeding than mothers of term babies. If you are anxious about feeding your baby he will be able to read this in your facial expressions and will become anxious himself. He will then be less likely to enjoy meals and food.

MINIMIZING LATER FEEDING DIFFICULTIES

As early as possible give your baby gentle touches around the mouth to show him that touches around the mouth can feel good too. For example, try gentle loving strokes of your baby's lips and around his mouth. You could also offer opportunities for comfort sucking. He will show you he would like to comfort suck by trying to bring his hands up to his mouth, turning his head and opening his mouth and by making little sucking movements.

As he gets older and you wean him, take particular care that you always make mealtimes pleasant and enjoyable.

- ▶ *Encourage him to try new tastes and textures by smiling at him and telling him it is going to be pleasant and fun.*
- ▶ *Always allow him to decide when he has had enough to eat. He will show you he has had enough in the same way term babies do (see page 37).*
- ▶ *Never force feed.*

END-OF-CHAPTER QUESTIONS

1 *How are preterm babies defined?*

2 *How many weeks early is a baby who has been born at 27 weeks' gestation?*

3 *For how long should preterm babies have their age corrected when their details are plotted on growth charts?*

4 *What are the main benefits of breast milk for preterm babies?*

5 *Why do preterm babies usually need to be fed via a tube?*

6 *About what age is a preterm baby ready to try suckling from his mother's nipple or a bottle teat?*

7 *Why do preterm babies need extra vitamin and mineral supplements?*

8 *When should you consider weaning a preterm baby?*

9 *What extra care do preterm babies need when being weaned?*

10 *Are preterm babies more or less likely than term babies to have feeding problems as toddlers?*

6

....

Healthy eating for over ones

In this chapter you will learn:
- *about choices of milk drinks*
- *the nutrients your baby needs to grow and stay healthy*
- *the food groups that make up a balanced diet*
- *the number of servings of each food group to offer each day*
- *how to organize a feeding routine around your baby's daytime sleeps.*

Once your baby is around one year old he should be eating almost all the family foods you do even though some foods will have to be cut up. He should also be feeding himself quite well with finger foods and may begin to use a spoon to try to feed himself.

In this second year of life he is still growing rapidly but his weight gain will be lower than that of babies under one. During this year he will only gain around 2.4 kg/5 lb compared with 6.6 kg/14½ lb during his first year. He will also grow more slowly – about 12 cm/ 5 in taller compared to 25 cm/10 in during his first year. However, his development will astound you as he masters walking and talking and begins to assert his own independence.

Comparison of babies' growth rates per year		
	Weight gain	Height increase
0–12 months	6.6 kg/14½ lb	25 cm/10 in
1–2 years	2.4 kg/5 lb	12 cm/5 in

> **Insight**
> Most parents do not realize how much growth slows down in
> the second year. They expect their babies to carry on gaining
> weight as quickly as they did during their first year and this
> causes a lot of unnecessary anxiety.

Over the year your baby will expend a lot more energy as
he becomes more mobile, investigating his environment and
developing his balance and co-ordination through play and physical
activity. He will use up some of the fat he stored before he began
walking. Over this year you should see him slim down a bit – this
is quite normal. Some parents worry unnecessarily that weight gain
is slower but, in fact, this slimming down is a very important part
of his development and toddlers normally carry on getting slimmer
and slimmer until they are about four or five years old.

If you are worried about your baby's weight ask your health visitor
to weigh and measure him and to plot these measurements on his
growth charts in his red book or Personal Child Health Record.
It is important that the measurements are taken on accurate
calibrated scales so it is best to have him measured at a health
clinic by healthcare professionals.

Food and drinks to offer

Now is the time to include your baby in as many family meals
as possible and give him the foods you are eating. You can now
include:

▶ *honey*
▶ *small amounts of foods which have been preserved with salt,
  such as bacon, and tinned foods. However, as a family it is
  best to avoid large amounts of processed foods that have extra
  added salt. Use herbs and spices to flavour foods rather than
  salt. Do not add salt to your baby's food at the table.*

Food to continue to avoid:

▶ *Very spicy food such as hot chilli.*
▶ *Undercooked eggs and shellfish – babies can become severely ill with food poisoning.*
▶ *Large fish that live for many years, such as shark, swordfish and marlin – these may contain high levels of mercury.*
▶ *Whole nuts – babies can react severely to them if they are inhaled. Babies may also choke on them.*
▶ *Tea – the tannin in tea reduces the amount of iron which your baby can absorb. It is best not to give tea to babies but if you do so, do not offer it with a meal.*
▶ *Additives and sweeteners – it is best to offer your baby foods without large amounts of additives or sweeteners. However, if your family foods include some keep them to a minimum for your baby. See page 232 for more information but do avoid the following:*

Colours:

Tartrazine E102
Ponceau 4 R E124
Sunset yellow E110
Carmosine E122
Quinoline yellow E104
Allura red AC E129.

Preservatives:

Sodium benzoate E211

Insight
Since the Food Standards Agency advised against children having these colourings, most companies have now removed them from their foods and drinks.

Cutting back on milk

The biggest difference for babies over one year is that they need less milk than babies under one. Milk is low in iron and babies who continue to drink too much milk in their second year may not eat enough iron-containing foods and could develop iron deficiency anaemia.

Instead of three to four milk-feeds of about 200 ml/7 fl oz each, now he only needs about three servings of milk, cheese and yogurt per day.

A serving is:

▶ *a cup of milk containing 100–120 ml/3–4 fl oz as a drink or on breakfast cereal.*
▶ *cheese in a sandwich or on top of pizza or pasta.*
▶ *a pot of yogurt.*
▶ *a serving of a milk pudding such as custard or rice pudding.*

Insight

I have seen many babies and toddlers with iron deficiency anaemia whose parents did not make this change around one year of age. The babies carried on drinking too much milk well into their second and third years – often large bottles of milk on waking in the morning, just before bedtime and during the night.

CHANGING THE BEDTIME ROUTINE TO CUT OUT THE LAST MILK-FEED

Sometime soon after your baby's first birthday it is time to cut out the last milk-feed at bedtime. He will now be able to sleep through the night without becoming hungry. Change the bedtime routine so that it does not include a milk-feed but do continue to spend some time with him to comfort him before he goes to bed:

- *Give him a bath.*
- *Dress him in his pyjamas.*
- *Cuddle him and spend some time looking at a book with him.*
- *Put him into his bed while he is still awake and say good night. Allow him to settle on his own with a comforter such as his favourite toy or a special cloth or blanket he may have chosen.*

Finishing with bottles

If he is still drinking from a bottle after his first birthday then change to all drinks from cups as quickly as you can. Babies who continue drinking from bottles into their second year tend to use bottle-drinking as a comforter and can become more stubborn about demanding it the older they become.

Continuing to drink from a bottle, particularly when it is used for comforting themselves, will mean a much longer contact time between the fluid and the teeth. For any drink other than water this can be a problem as they all contain some sugar. Milk contains lactose as sugar, fruit juices contain the fruit sugar fructose and squashes contain the sugars glucose and sucrose. Both fruit juices and squashes also contain acid which causes tooth enamel to erode.

Changing the milk drink

From 12 months, cows' milk can be used as the milk drink instead of breast milk or formula milk. There is, however, no hurry to change. One advantage of cows' milk is that it is cheaper than formula milks. It is also higher in protein and is quite suitable for babies over one year who are eating well. There are a range of growing-up milks as alternatives to cows' milk for babies over one year.

The choice of milk drink for babies from 12 months old

▶ *You can change to cows' milk.*
▶ *You can continue with the breast milk, formula milk or follow-on milk they are currently drinking.*
▶ *You can change to a growing-up milk.*

COWS' MILK

Whole cows' milk is very suitable as the main milk drink for babies over 12 months of age. Semi-skimmed cows' milk is not recommended for babies under two years of age and skimmed milk should not be used for children under five years of age. This is because they are lower in fat and lower in the important fat-soluble vitamin A which is needed for his growth and development.

FOLLOW-ON MILKS

These have more iron and some other nutrients than breast milk and cows' milk. They can be useful for babies over 12 months when a healthcare professional or mother is concerned that the baby's food intake is poor for any reason.

GROWING-UP MILKS

These milks are promoted as being suitable up to three years. They contain less protein than cows' milk but more vitamins and minerals, particularly iron and zinc. If a baby is eating well then they will be getting these vitamins and minerals from their food so the extra expense is not necessarily justified. However, they will provide useful extra nutrients for a baby or young toddler who eats poorly. There are now five on the market and they are fairly similar, although one is based on goats' milk rather than cows' milk:

Aptamil Growing-Up Milk
Cow & Gate Growing-Up Milk

Hipp Organic Growing-Up milk
Nanny Care Goat Milk-based Growing-Up Milk
SMA Toddler Milk

....
Insight

After your baby's first birthday, milk makes a much smaller
contribution to the overall diet than it did during the first
year, so it does not really matter whether you give your
baby cows', follow-on or growing-up milk. All of them
provide approximately the same amount of calcium, iodine
and B vitamins, which are the nutrients your baby needs
from milk.
....

OTHER DRINKS

Busy, active babies can get quite thirsty and need several drinks
each day. As they are now drinking less milk remember to
offer drinks with each meal and in between. Babies can become
dehydrated quite quickly in hot weather or if they have a
temperature or a runny nose. As your baby will not be able to
tell you if he is thirsty, always offer a drink of water if he is crying
for no other apparent reason. He will push it away if he does not
want it.

Offer about six to eight drinks per day – each about 100–120 ml/
3–4 fl oz. Too little fluid can cause constipation.

Milk and water are the safest drinks to offer between meals as they
do not harm teeth. Diluted fruit juices can be given with meals but
should not be offered between meals as they are acidic and contain
fruit sugar. Any sugar, including fruit sugar, will decay teeth if
offered frequently and acid can cause your baby's delicate tooth
enamel to erode.

Other sugary drinks such as fruit juice drinks and squashes have
no place in a baby's diet as they just contribute sugar with no other
nutrients. They are also acidic.

For a nutritious balanced diet, think food groups not nutrients

Now that your baby is relying more on food and less on milk for his nutrients it is important to offer him a good combination of nutritious foods to provide the full range of nutrients he needs.

Insight

I was surprised to learn from one survey that some mothers give sweetened drinks rather than water to their babies because they think that giving tasteless water is cruel. However, most babies happily drink water and giving sweet, acidic drinks that increase the likelihood of dental decay for the baby can be seen as cruel.

Babies over one are still growing and developing at a fast pace compared to older children and to support this growth they need more energy and nutrients per kilogram of their body weight than adults. They need about 95 Kcalories for every kilogram (2¼ lb) they weigh, whereas adults only need about one third of this – that is about 30–35 Kcalories for every kilogram (2¼ lb) they weigh. As babies stomachs are quite small they need very nutritious foods at all meals.

To get these relatively large amounts of calories and nutrients into small stomachs it is important not to give babies of this age only the low-fat, high-fibre foods which are recommended for a healthy balanced diet for older children and adults. Too many high-fibre foods could reduce the amount of food, and therefore energy and nutrients that they eat.

Two to three nutritious snacks in addition to three meals each day will help to give your baby the calories and nutrients he needs.

The nutrients he needs are:

▶ *Protein*
▶ *Carbohydrate*

- ▶ *Fat*
- ▶ *Fibre*
- ▶ *Vitamins:* *Vitamin A and carotene which is a form of vitamin A*

  B vitamins which include thiamine, folic acid, niacin (nicotinamide), riboflavin, pyridoxine, biotin, pantothenic acid and vitamin B12

  Vitamin C which is ascorbic acid

  Vitamin D

  Vitamin E

  Vitamin K
- ▶ *Minerals:* *Calcium*

  Copper

  Fluoride

  Iodine

  Iron

  Magnesium

  Phosphorus

  Potassium

  Selenium

  Sodium

  Zinc
- ▶ *Phytonutrients: These are substances in plants which boost the immune system and provide long-term protection against cancer and heart disease. They include the brightly coloured pigments in fruits and vegetables and are also called flavanoids, flavanols and isoflavones.*

It is not necessary for you to worry about how much of each nutrient you are feeding your toddler because experts have grouped foods into food groups and all the foods within each food group provide a similar range of certain nutrients. There are four nutritious food groups and if you combine these food groups as recommended on pages 131–133, your baby will automatically be getting roughly the right amount of nutrients. Within each food group you need to offer as much variety as your baby is happy to eat.

As before, allow your baby to eat according to his appetite rather than to specific serving sizes. The amounts babies eat varies from baby to baby – some eat much more or much less than average intakes, and yet grow and develop normally. The amount babies eat also varies from day to day but if you always offer nutritious foods when he eats well he will be getting plenty of nutrients.

The four nutritious food groups are:

1 *Bread, rice, potatoes, pasta and other starchy foods*
2 *Fruit and vegetables*
3 *Milk, cheese and yogurt*
4 *Meat, fish, eggs, nuts and pulses.*

In addition there is a fifth food group of foods high in either fat, sugar or both. These provide fewer nutrients and are high in energy (calories). They can be included in smaller quantities but should not replace foods in the food groups 1–4.

The nutrients which each food group provides are as follows:

Food group	Foods included	Main nutrients supplied
1. Bread, rice, potatoes, pasta and other starchy foods	Bread, chapatti, breakfast cereals, rice, couscous, pasta, millet, potatoes, yam and foods made with flour, such as pizza bases, buns, pancakes, scones	Carbohydrate B vitamins Fibre Some iron, zinc and calcium
2. Fruit and vegetables	Fresh, frozen, tinned and dried fruits and vegetables. Also pure fruit juices	Vitamin C Potassium Phytochemicals Fibre Carotenes, which are a form of vitamin A

Food group	Foods included	Main nutrients supplied
3. Milk, cheese and yogurt	Breast milk, infant formulas, follow-on milks, cows' milk, yogurts, cheese, calcium-enriched soy milks, tofu	Calcium Phosphorus Protein Iodine Riboflavin
4. Meat, fish, eggs, nuts and pulses	Meat, fish, eggs, nuts and pulses, e.g. lentils, dhal, chickpeas, humous, kidney beans and other similar starchy beans	Iron Protein Zinc Magnesium B vitamins Vitamin A Omega 3 and omega 6 fats Omega 3 long-chain fatty acids: EPA and DHA from oily fish
Foods high in fat	Cream, butter, margarines, cooking and salad oils, mayonnaise	Some foods provide: Vitamins D and E Omega 3 and omega 6 fats
Foods high in sugar	Jam, honey, syrup, confectionery	Sugar
Foods high in fat and sugar	Ice cream, biscuits, cakes, chocolate	Sugar Fat Small amounts of some vitamins and minerals

COMBINING FOOD GROUPS FOR A NUTRITIOUS, BALANCED DIET

The recommendations that follow will give you a guide as to how much to offer your baby each day as part of your feeding routine. However, there is no need to worry if there are days when this combination doesn't happen. Babies store nutrients, so if they don't eat well for a few days they will come to no harm. As long as they are getting a good balance of the four food groups, with some variety within each group, then they are doing well.

1. Bread, rice, potatoes, pasta and other starchy foods

This group includes all types of bread, chapatti, pasta, rice, couscous, potatoes, sweet potatoes, yam, green banana, breakfast cereals and foods made from flour and other cereals such as rye, millet and sorghum. Offer a mixture of some white and some wholegrain varieties as all wholegrain foods would provide too much fibre for a baby.

Recommendation: Include one of these foods at each meal and also offer them at some snack times, for example:

▶ *Breakfast – breakfast cereals, porridge, bread, toast or chapatti.*
▶ *Lunch and evening meal – potatoes, rice, pasta, couscous, bread, chapatti, yam or green banana.*
▶ *Snacks – bread, bread sticks, rice cakes or crackers, other foods based on flour such as pancakes, currant buns, tea bread and scones.*

2. Fruit and vegetables

This group includes raw, cooked and dried fruit and vegetables.

Recommendation: Serve them at each meal. The more variety the better.

▶ *Serve fruit at breakfast and at least one vegetable and one fruit at lunch and the evening meal.*
▶ *Set a good example by eating fruit and vegetables yourself.*
▶ *Cut raw fruit and vegetables into slices, cubes or sticks as babies find these easier to eat than a large, whole fruit.*
▶ *Remove any pips or stones but babies should be able to manage the skin on fruits such as apples, pears, peaches, grapes, etc.*
▶ *Babies often prefer the flavour of vegetables that have been stir fried, roasted or baked rather than boiled.*
▶ *Dried fruit should not be given as snacks as it sticks to teeth and can cause tooth decay in the same way sweets do. However, you can include them as part of a meal.*

3. Milk, cheese and yogurt

This group includes dairy foods such as milk, cheese and yogurt. Milk on breakfast cereal or as milk puddings or white sauces is also included.

Recommendation: Serve about three times a day. Milk may be taken as a drink or poured onto breakfast cereal. Always use whole or full fat milk products for babies.

One serving is:

- *about 120 ml/4 fl oz glass or cup of milk*
- *about 120 g/4 oz pot of full fat yogurt or fromage frais*
- *a serving of cheese in a sandwich or on top of a pizza slice*
- *a serving of custard or another milk pudding made with whole milk*
- *a serving of food in a white cheese sauce such as macaroni cheese.*

4. Meat, fish, eggs, nuts and pulses

This group includes the richest sources of iron in the diet – meat, fish, eggs, nuts and pulses. Pulses include starchy beans like kidney beans (not green beans), chickpeas, humous, lentils and dhal. When eggs, pulses and nuts are served, a food or drink high in vitamin C should also be included in the meal to ensure good absorption of iron.

Recommendation: Serve once or twice a day for non-vegetarians and two or three times a day for vegetarians.

- *Most babies prefer softer cuts of meat such as chicken, minced meat, sausages, paté or slowly baked meat. Some find it difficult to eat the hard, chewy textures of less tender meat and will refuse it. Choose sausages and minced meat products such as burgers with a high lean meat content and low fat content to make sure adequate levels of nutrients are provided.*
- *Vegetarian alternatives include eggs, ground or chopped nuts and pulses such as beans, chickpeas, humous, lentils and dhal. To aid the absorption of iron, these need to be served with high vitamin C foods such as tomatoes, peppers, citrus fruits, kiwi fruit, strawberries, pineapple and potato. Diluted fruit juices high in vitamin C such as blackcurrant or citrus juices can also be served with the meal.*

> **Care with nuts**
>
> Do not use whole nuts as they could be inhaled or may cause choking. Nut butters and ground or chopped nuts in recipes are fine.

Foods high in fat

Oils, butter and margarine provide babies with energy from the fat and can also provide key nutrients such as omega 3 and omega 6 fats and the vitamins A and E depending on the oils or fat used.

Recommendation: Offer these foods in small amounts in addition to, but not instead of, foods from the other four food groups.

- ▶ *Use rapeseed oil for cooking as it is high in omega 3 fatty acids.*
- ▶ *Olive oil, soya oil and walnut oil have a good balance of omega 3 and 6 fats and can be used in dressings. Olive and soya oil can also be used in cooking.*
- ▶ *Butter and margarines can also be used in cooking or as spreads on bread. Margarines are fortified with vitamins A and D by law but choose one with a low level of trans fats as there is now concern about the large amounts of these in our food.*
- ▶ *Crisps and other similar snacks are also included in this group. They are usually high in salt as well as fat and provide few other nutrients. They have no place in a baby's diet on a regular basis. If you give them to your baby just give him a few occasionally – certainly not a whole packet.*

Foods high in sugar

- ▶ *Your baby will soon learn that sweets and other confectionery have a sweet taste which all babies naturally enjoy. However, they offer very few other nutrients other than sugar so should be given occasionally if at all. However, well-meaning grandparents and friends may bring them as presents even if you do not buy them. Get into the habit of putting them away in a box and give them occasionally as part of a pudding. Never use them as rewards or bribes.*

- *Honey and jam have a few nutrients other than sugar and small amounts can be used to add flavour and a little sweetness.*
- *Sweetened drinks are also in this group. They are not recommended for babies but if you give them, dilute them well and only offer them with food at a meal to lessen their tendency to cause dental decay and erosion of tooth enamel.*

Foods high in fat and sugar
- *Cake, biscuits and ice cream all contain some nutrients other than just sugar and fat and can be combined with fruit as a second course or pudding at mealtimes.*

Vitamin supplements

If you have not already started vitamin drops, now is the time to start. Babies all need vitamin drops containing vitamins A and D. Breastfed babies need to start at six months and babies on formula milk need to start when they are having less than 500 ml/17 fl oz formula which will be from about 11 to 12 months old.

Babies have high needs for both these vitamins at this time and will not necessarily get enough from their food. This is particularly important for babies:

- *with dark skins – that is, those of Asian, African, Afro-Caribbean and Middle-Eastern origin – because they do not make vitamin D in their skins as efficiently as white babies*
- *who live in northern areas of the UK where there is less sunlight to make vitamin D*
- *who were born prematurely*
- *who are on restricted diets such as vegetarian diets*
- *who are picky, fussy eaters.*

Insight

I find many parents are not aware of the need for these supplements as GPs and health visitors do not readily give this advice. However, it has been a public health policy in the UK since 1991.

Food group	Recommendation
1. Bread, rice, potatoes, pasta and other starchy foods	Serve one of these foods at each meal.
2. Fruit and vegetables	Serve fruit at breakfast, and at least one vegetable and one fruit at the midday and evening meals.
3. Milk, cheese and yogurt	Serve about three times a day.
4. Meat, fish, eggs, nuts and pulses	Serve two to three times per day.
Foods high in fat and/or sugar	Offer in small amounts. They should not replace foods from the other food groups.
Vitamin supplement	One dose containing vitamins A and D each day.

Textures and flavours

In this second year your baby will have established some quite definite likes and dislikes in terms of flavour and texture of foods. Some babies like their food bathed in sauces while others prefer it dry and some like every food kept separate from the others on the plate. Many do not like stringy meat or foods that are difficult to chew. Bear this in mind and don't insist your baby eats something he is not enjoying as this will create a negative association with that food. With time his tastes and preferences may change so it is important to keep offering him all the foods you and your family are eating. However, make sure there is always something that he enjoys eating at each meal.

Looking after teeth

Your baby will be getting more teeth during this year. Although they are first teeth and they will eventually be replaced by permanent teeth, taking care of these first teeth is extremely important. They are necessary for the development of the jaw so that it is able to accommodate the permanent teeth when they come in from around six years of age. Good dental hygiene at this age involves brushing the teeth that are there twice a day with a smear of fluoride toothpaste on a soft brush. You will have to do this for your baby but encourage him to try himself. You can finish off to make sure it has been done well. Sugary food can cause decay and acidic drinks will erode delicate tooth enamel so only offer them at mealtimes.

Insight

Brushing your baby's teeth can be a tricky business, but he will enjoy it more when it becomes a fun part of his routine.

Avoiding excess calories and obesity

With increasing numbers of toddlers becoming overweight and obese there seems to be a fine balance to strike between not giving them enough food to provide all their nutrients and energy for growth and giving them too much so that they become overweight. However, observing a few simple rules will make sure you do not set up a lifestyle pattern to cause overweight or obesity problems.

▶ *Allow your baby to eat to his appetite and never insist he finishes everything on his plate.*
▶ *Do not coerce him to eat more when he has shown you he has had enough.*
▶ *Always combine some low-calorie foods with high-calorie foods at each meal. Fruit and vegetables are low-calorie foods so always make these part of every meal.*
▶ *Do not use food as a reward.*

- *Keep food to set meals and snacks rather than allowing grazing between meals and planned snacks.*
- *Offer water rather than any sweetened drinks, including fruit juices, between meals and snacks.*
- *Allow him plenty of opportunity for active play each day. If you do not have a garden for him to play in then take him to a playground each day. Let him walk when he wants to even though this will slow you down – do not insist he always sits in his stroller or car seat when you are out and about.*

Encouraging a positive attitude to food and meals

Some time during this second year your baby will begin to become wary of new foods and may go through a phase of seeming fussy and faddy about foods. It is a normal part of his development (see Chapter 8) and he will now take much longer to learn to like new foods:

- *He may need to watch others eating a food that is new to him several times before he becomes confident to try it himself.*
- *He may take much longer to learn to like that food and he will do this by just tasting a little each time you include it in a meal. It is the number of times he tastes that food not the amount he eats that will determine how long before he learns to like the food.*

Try to remember it is up to you to offer your baby nutritious food but up to your baby to decide which foods he will eat and how much he will eat of each one. He will be telling you he has had enough food when he:

- *says no*
- *keeps his mouth shut when food is offered*
- *turns his head away from the food being offered*
- *pushes away the spoon, bowl or plate containing food*
- *holds food in his mouth and refuses to swallow it*
- *spits food out*
- *cries, shouts or screams*

▶ *tries to climb out of his highchair*
▶ *gags or retches.*

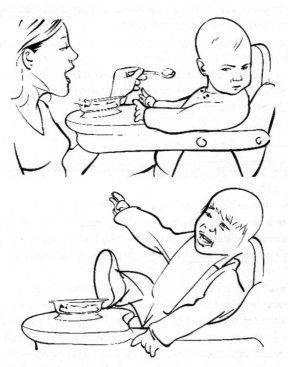

Figure 6.1 Signs that your baby has had enough to eat: turning his head away, screaming and trying to climb out of his chair.

Keep an open mind about how much your baby needs to eat – he knows this better than you do. Make each meal a pleasant and sociable occasion that you, your baby and the rest of the family enjoy:

▶ *Eat together as a family as often as possible.*
▶ *Limit mealtimes to suit the attention span of your baby – about 20 minutes is enough.*
▶ *Eat in a calm, relaxed manner if possible without distractions such as TV, games and toys so that your baby can concentrate on eating.*
▶ *Allow your baby plenty of control over how much and what he eats by giving him finger foods to feed himself and allow*

him to try spoon-feeding himself. You will still need to help feed him.

▶ *Give your baby attention when he is eating and praise him for having eaten well when he finishes.*

Insight

Parents find that not coercing their baby to eat more is one of the hardest things to do – particularly when the parents have lovingly prepared the food themselves.

Learning through investigating the environment and playing

Babies are learning all the time through playing. When dropping things they will notice that they fall to the floor, thus learning about the law of gravity. Sitting in a highchair is an ideal opportunity to watch objects, including food, fall to the ground. Although this will involve mess, try to see it through your baby's eyes – he is investigating and learning and not deliberately trying to make a mess for you to clear up. Try not to scold severely even though it is obviously an activity you will need to discourage. Try to keep meals pleasant and not a time when you are excessively scolding.

Figure 6.2 Babies are learning all the time – even when they make a mess for you to clean up. Remember, they are not doing this deliberately.

Meal and snack routines

A regular pattern of meals and snacks has advantages because babies:

▶ *love ritual, routine and predictability – it helps them to feel safe and content*
▶ *do not eat well if they are tired or over hungry.*

Now your baby is mobile he will be busy and active and can become tired very quickly. Organize a feeding routine around his daytime sleeps so that you are not feeding him when he is tired or has gone too long without eating so that he is over hungry. Snacks evenly spaced between meals will help to avoid the frustrations of being over hungry.

Give both a savoury and sweet course at meals. This gives two opportunities for nutrients to be consumed and increases the variety of foods he is eating. Nutritious puddings are a valuable part of the meal and should not be used only as a reward for eating the savoury course.

Insight
Parents tell me that they are afraid their baby will refuse the savoury course and just wait for the pudding if they follow this advice. This fear is unfounded as babies will happily eat the savoury course if they are familiar with the foods being offered and they like them. Puddings should always be limited to just one serving.

DAILY FEEDING ROUTINE

During their second year some babies will continue with two daytime sleeps while others may just have one.

With one daytime sleep

Early morning:	Wakes – no milk-feed.
7 a.m. breakfast:	Cereal and milk and fruit or egg and toast with fruit juice.
	Cup of milk.
9:30 a.m.	Snack and drink.
12:30 p.m. light lunch:	Savoury course.
	Fruit.
	Water in a cup with the meal.
1:30 p.m. sleep for one to two hours	
3:30 p.m.	Snack and cup of milk.
6 p.m. tea:	Savoury course.
	Milk-based pudding with fruit.
	Water in a cup with the meal.

Bedtime routine – no milk-feed.

With two daytime sleeps

Early morning:	Wakes – no milk-feed.
7 a.m. breakfast:	Cereal and milk and fruit or egg and toast with fruit juice.
	Cup of milk.
9:30 a.m.	Snack and drink.
10:30 a.m. sleep for about an hour	
12:00 a.m. lunch:	Savoury course.
	Milk-based pudding with fruit.
	Water in a cup with the meal.
2:30 p.m. sleep for about an hour	
4:00 p.m.	Snack and drink.
6:30 p.m. tea:	Savoury course.
	Cake-style pudding with fruit.
	Water in a cup with the meal.
	Finish with a cup of milk.

Bedtime routine – no milk-feed.

Menu plans

Time	Course	Day 1	Day 2	Day 3
Breakfast		Porridge with milk Banana slices	Boiled egg with toast fingers Kiwi fruit slices	Breakfast wheat biscuit with blueberries and milk
Midday meal	First course	Chicken nuggets with roasted vegetables	Fish fingers with sweet potato and broccoli	Mini meatballs with potato wedges and cauliflower florets
	Second course	Fromage frais and pear slices	Banana with custard	Yogurt and fruit slices
	Drinks	Water	Water	Water
Evening meal	First course	Mushroom omelette with toast fingers and cherry tomatoes	Pasta and red pepper sauce with grated cheese	Mini pizza with carrot and cucumber sticks
	Second course	Fruit salad with ice cream	Mini muffin and fruit slices	Drop scones with raspberries
	Drinks	Water and milk-feed to finish	Water and milk-feed to finish	Water and milk-feed to finish

Examples of snacks – always offer a drink as well

▶ *Slices of fruit with a small cup of milk.*
▶ *Small sandwich and a cup of water.*
▶ *Slices of apple, spread with cream cheese and cup of water.*
▶ *Pancakes, spread with fruit purée or chocolate spread and cup of water.*
▶ *Breadsticks or crackers with cubes of cheese and cup of water.*
▶ *Pitta bread with humous or cream cheese and cup of water.*
▶ *Muffin with a small cup of milk.*
▶ *Crumpet, spread with honey and cup of water.*
▶ *Scone and cup of milk.*
▶ *Yogurt or fromage frais and fruit slices and cup of water.*
▶ *Small piece cake and cup of milk.*
▶ *Small slice of pizza and cup of water.*
▶ *Small bowl of breakfast cereal and milk.*

Recipes combining the food groups

Continue to use any recipes your baby enjoyed when he was younger but include him in as many family meals as you can, offering him the same foods you are eating. You will need to continue helping to feed him but he will increasingly feed himself with his fingers and his own spoon. He will enjoy being in control of his own eating when feeding himself. Regularly serve him foods he can eat with his fingers.

1 BREAKFASTS

Microwaved porridge with apricots
A quickly prepared, hot breakfast with sweet chewy apricots makes a great start to the day.

5 tbsp porridge oats
4 dried apricots, diced
90 ml/3 fl oz milk
90 ml/3 fl oz water

Put the oats and chopped apricots in a wide soup bowl and pour the milk and water in. Microwave on full power, uncovered, for three minutes. Stir thoroughly and allow to stand to cool a little. Serve with extra milk or yogurt.

Makes 1–2 servings.

Muesli
3 tbsp rolled oats
1 tbsp wheatgerm
1 tbsp ground almonds
2 tbsp dried fruit – sultanas, raisins or chopped apricots
1 tbsp dessicated coconut
1 tsp brown sugar

Mix all the ingredients together. Serve with milk or yogurt and some extra fresh fruit if desired.

Makes 1–2 servings.

2 MEAT

Homemade chicken nuggets
It's so easy to make these chicken nuggets that look similar to commercially produced nuggets but are superior in quality and nutrients. They are also lower in salt. You can make your own breadcrumbs or use fine, dried breadcrumbs available in the supermarkets.

½ chicken breast
1 egg, beaten
3 tbsp dried breadcrumbs
½ tsp dried mixed herbs

Preheat the oven to 200°C/400°F/gas mark 6. Lightly grease a non-stick oven tray by brushing with olive oil. Cut the chicken breast into small strips. Put the beaten egg in one small bowl. Mix the breadcrumbs and herbs in a separate small bowl. Dip the chicken breast strips into the egg and then into the breadcrumbs. Place each nugget on the baking tray. Cook in the oven for 10–15 minutes until golden and cooked through, turning once to brown both sides. Serve with oven roasted vegetable sticks.

Makes 2–4 servings.

Mini meatballs
1 small onion, peeled and cut into quarters
1 medium carrot, finely grated
2 tbsp breadcrumbs
1 tbsp tomato purée
1 tsp oregano or mixed herbs
½ tsp freshly ground black pepper
1 egg, whisked
200 g/7 oz lean minced beef

Preheat the oven to 180°C/350°F/gas mark 4. Put the onion pieces in a food processor and process until finely minced. Add in the carrot, breadcrumbs, tomato purée, mixed herbs, pepper and egg. Process for about ten seconds. Lastly, add in the minced beef and process for a further ten seconds until you have a finely ground mixture like sausage meat. Form meatballs about the size of a walnut and place them on a baking tray. Put into the oven for 25–30 minutes. Check they are cooked right through. Serve them with the tomato and red pepper sauce in the recipe below and either potato wedges or pasta shapes for an all finger food meal.

Makes 16 meatballs.

Tomato and red pepper sauce
This sauce is for accompanying the meatballs above but can also be used for pasta or chicken.

1 tbsp olive oil
½ onion, finely sliced
1 red or green pepper, deseeded and diced
1 clove garlic, crushed or thinly sliced
1 can (400 g/14 oz) chopped tomatoes

1 tsp oregano or basil
pinch freshly ground black pepper

Heat the oil in a frying pan and add the onion. Fry gently for a
few minutes then add the diced pepper and garlic. Continue frying
over a gently heat for another five minutes. Add the tomatoes,
herbs and pepper and simmer until the onions and pepper are soft.
Purée the sauce and keep warm to serve with chicken, pasta or
mini meatballs.

3 FISH

Homemade fish fingers
These are quick and easy to make and contain more fish than
commercial frozen fish fingers.

110 g/4 oz fillet white fish, e.g. cod or haddock
1 egg, beaten
4 tbsp dried breadcrumbs
1 tbsp rapeseed oil

Cut the fish into four pieces, taking off the skin and checking
carefully for any remaining bones. Put the egg in one bowl and
the breadcrumbs into another shallow bowl. Heat the oil in a
frying pan. Dip the fish pieces first in the egg, then coat all sides
with breadcrumbs and place into the hot oil. Fry for four to five
minutes, turning once, or until the fish is cooked right through and
the breadcrumbs are golden brown. Serve with mashed potato and
steamed vegetable sticks.

Makes 2–4 servings.

Salmon fingers
110 g/4 oz salmon fillet, skin removed
4 tbsp dried breadcrumbs
1 egg, beaten
1 clove garlic, peeled and crushed
2 tsp butter

Preheat the oven to 200°C/400°F/gas mark 6. Cut the salmon into fingers and check there are no bones. Beat the egg in a small bowl and put the breadcrumbs in another shallow bowl. Dip the salmon pieces in the egg and then coat in breadcrumbs. Place on a lightly greased baking tray. Mix together the crushed garlic and butter. Dot each piece of salmon with a little of the butter mixture. Bake in the oven for five to six minutes and then turn the salmon fingers and cook for a further four to five minutes until golden brown and cooked through. Do not overcook.

Makes 4 servings.

Mini fishcakes
These work well with smoked, oily fish but you can use white fish for a milder taste.

220 g/8 oz potato, peeled and cut into pieces
140g/5 oz fillets of smoked mackerel, trout or eel
1 egg, beaten
juice of 1 lemon
2 tbsp fresh chives or parsley, finely chopped
pinch pepper

Steam or boil the potatoes until tender. Place the smoked fish in a bowl and flake with a fork. Tip in the cooked potatoes, chives and pepper, and mash all together until well mixed. Add in the juice of half the lemon and just enough whisked egg to make a mixture that binds well but isn't too runny. Mix well. Form fish balls with a heaped dessertspoon of mixture and place on a grill pan lined with a sheet of aluminium foil. Your fingers will get quite sticky. Place under a hot grill, turning once, until golden brown (about five minutes either side). Drizzle with lemon juice before serving.

Makes 8 servings.

Tuna pasta
90 g/3 oz penne or other pasta shapes
½ small onion, peeled and finely chopped

1 garlic clove, peeled and crushed
2 tsp tomato purée
1 large ripe tomato chopped or ½ tin chopped tomatoes
110 g/4 oz tinned tuna in oil, drained (keep the oil)

Cook the penne or pasta in boiling water according to instructions on the packet. Meanwhile, put the drained oil from the tinned tuna in a small pan over a gentle heat. Fry the onion and garlic until soft – about ten minutes. Add the tomato purée and tomatoes. Simmer for two to three minutes. Flake the tuna and add. Continue simmering for another two minutes. Drain the pasta when cooked and add to the tomato sauce. Serve with some vegetable sticks.

Makes 2–4 servings.

4 VEGETABLES

Stir-frying or roasting vegetables gives them a more attractive flavour than steaming or boiling. Always wash them well.

Stir-fried vegetable sticks
1 tbsp olive oil
3 small broccoli florets
3 small cauliflower florets
4 baby corn, halved or left whole if they are small
4 mangetout, topped and tailed
4 button mushrooms
½ red pepper, cored, deseeded and sliced lengthways

Heat the oil in a non-stick frying pan. Add the cauliflower and broccoli florets first and cook for a couple of minutes. Then add the baby corn, mangetout, mushrooms and pepper slices. Stir the vegetables from time to time to stop them burning on one side. Continue cooking for another five to eight minutes until the vegetables are slightly softened but still al dente. Serve with any of the savoury dishes.

Makes 2–4 servings.

5 TEA DISHES

Mushroom omelette
1 egg
½ tbsp water
small pinch pepper
1 tsp butter or oil
2 button mushrooms, thinly sliced

Using a fork, beat the egg and water with the pepper in a small
bowl. Melt the butter in a small non-stick frying pan and add
the mushroom slices and sauté until softened. Remove from the
pan. Add a little more butter to the pan and allow it to melt and
cover the base, then turn up the heat. Once the butter is sizzling,
pour in the egg mixture and add the mushrooms to one half of
the egg mixture. Cook over a medium to high heat until the egg is
cooked through. Fold the half without mushrooms over the half
with mushrooms. Cut into finger size pieces for your baby to feed
himself. Serve with toast fingers.

Tortilla
This is a complete savoury course containing egg, potato and
vegetables all together.

2 tsp rapeseed oil
1 spring onion, finely chopped
1 medium potato (about 100 g/4 oz), peeled, diced and steamed
2 tbsp diced fresh vegetables that have been cooked, or use frozen
mixed vegetables
2 eggs, beaten
2 tbsp grated cheese

Heat the oil in a small non-stick frying pan. Add the spring
onion, potatoes and vegetables and fry over a gentle heat, stirring
occasionally, until potatoes are slightly brown and vegetables are
hot (about six to eight minutes). Sprinkle in the grated cheese and
then pour in the beaten eggs. Carry on cooking without stirring
until the underside is cooked. Place the pan under a preheated
grill until the top is golden brown and the eggs are cooked all the

way through. Lift the tortilla onto a chopping board and slice into fingers or triangles.

Makes 2–4 servings.

Sandwich fillings and toast toppings
Any of these fillings can be used to make sandwiches or spread on toast, crackers or rice cakes:

▶ *1 tbsp cream cheese with ½ tsp chopped chives*
▶ *1 tbsp cream cheese with a scrape of marmite*
▶ *½ tbsp smooth peanut butter with ½ tbsp mashed banana*
▶ *1 tbsp humous and ½ tbsp finely diced red pepper*
▶ *1 tbsp drained tinned tuna with 1 tsp mayonnaise and 1 tsp plain yogurt*

Toast fingers with chicken liver paté
55 g/2 oz chicken livers
15 g/½ oz butter
2 spring onions, chopped
1 tsp chopped thyme
½ celery stick, chopped
½ tbsp apple juice
2 slices thick white bread

Melt the butter in a non-stick frying pan. Sauté the spring onion for a few minutes. Trim and chop the chicken livers and add in with the thyme, celery and apple juice. Cook for a further 10–12 minutes, stirring often. The livers should be cooked right through and the vegetables soft. Remove from the heat and mash together with a fork or use a blender for a smoother texture. Toast the bread and spread with the paté. Cut into fingers and serve with cherry tomatoes or slices of cucumber.

Makes 2–3 servings.

Toast fingers with oily fish
25 g/1 oz smoked mackerel or tinned sardines/pilchards in oil and well drained

½ tbsp natural bio yogurt
½ tsp lemon juice
½ tsp tomato purée
2 slices thick white or brown bread

Mash the fish with the yogurt, lemon juice and tomato purée. Toast the bread and spread with the fish mixture. If you wish to serve it warm, place under a preheated grill for one to two minutes. Cut into fingers and serve with vegetable sticks.

Makes 2–4 servings.

Mini pizzas
It takes minutes to put these pizzas together and you can vary the toppings.

Ham and pepper pizza

1 mini pitta bread
½ tbsp tomato purée
pinch dried oregano
1 slice of ham, diced
3 thin slices courgette, cubed
½ red pepper, cored, deseeded and diced
1 tbsp grated parmesan cheese
1 tbsp grated cheddar cheese

Preheat the grill. Spread the tomato purée over one side of the pitta bread. Sprinkle over the oregano and then scatter the ham, courgette and pepper pieces evenly over the top. Lastly sprinkle on the two cheeses. Grill for five minutes or until the cheeses have melted and are just beginning to brown. Cool and cut into slices or triangles for serving.

Mushroom and pepper pizza

1 mini pitta bread
½ tbsp tomato purée
1 small button mushroom, sliced

½ green pepper, cored, deseeded and diced
2 tbsp grated mozzarella cheese

Spread the tomato purée on one side of the pitta bread. Sprinkle on the mushroom and pepper followed by the cheese and the oregano. Cook under a hot grill for two to three minutes until the cheese is bubbling. Cool and cut into slices for serving.

Makes 1 serving.

6 PUDDINGS

Fruit salad for summer days
These summer fruits are at their best in July and August.

1 ripe peach
1 ripe apricot
1 wedge of melon
4 strawberries
6 blueberries

Wash the peach, apricot and berries. Cut the peach and apricot in half and remove the stones. Most babies will be happy eating these two fruits with the skin left on but some may prefer them peeled. Cut the fruit into bite-size pieces. Deseed the melon wedge, remove the rind and cut the remainder into bite-size pieces. Remove the stalks from the berries and mix the fruits together. Serve on their own or with a small scoop of ice cream.

Makes 1 serving for your baby and one for you.

Fruit salad for autumn days
All these fruits are in season and at their best in October and November. This makes a refreshing dessert to follow a warm meal. Some toddlers will prefer it on its own but it can be served with fromage frais or yogurt.

1 satsuma
1 ripe pear

4 blackberries or loganberries
4 small seedless grapes

Peel the satsuma and divide into segments. If there are pips, cut the segments in half and remove the pips. Wash the rest of the fruit well. Core the pear and cut into bite-size cubes. Mix all the fruits together in a bowl.

Makes 1 serving for your baby and one for you.

Tropical finger fruit salad
½ small ripe mango
1 wedge of melon
1 ripe kiwi fruit
1 slice of fresh pineapple
Few slices of banana

Peel the mango and kiwi fruit. Cut the fruit into bite-size pieces. Cut away the rind and hard core from the pineapple slice. Cut the remainder into bite-size pieces. Deseed the melon wedge, remove the rind and cut into small pieces. Mix all the fruit together.

Makes 1 serving for your baby and one for you.

Drop scones
2 eggs
1 tbsp sugar
120 ml/4 fl oz milk
110 g/4 oz self-raising flour
1 tsp baking powder
1 tbsp butter, melted
butter for frying

Put the eggs and the sugar in a bowl and beat with a whisk until they are thick. Add the milk, flour, baking powder and melted butter and beat until smooth. Leave the mixture to stand for at least ten minutes.

Melt a little butter on a large flat non-stick pan. Drop heaped tablespoons of batter into the pan to make small rounds, well spaced apart. Allow them to cook until bubbles appear on the surface and burst. Turn them over and cook for a further one to two minutes until they are golden brown on both sides. You will need to make several batches until all the mixture is used.

Serve them with fruit fingers or topped with a thick fruit purée.

Makes about 24 little scones.

Mini sultana muffins
85 g/3 oz wholemeal flour
130 g/5 oz plain white flour
100 g/3½ oz sultanas
3 tsp baking powder
50 g/2 oz soft dark brown sugar
45 g/1½ oz butter, melted
1 egg, beaten
250 ml/8 fl oz milk

Preheat the oven to 200°C/400°F/gas mark 6. Mix together all the dry ingredients in a bowl. Beat the egg and add the butter and milk. Pour the wet ingredients onto the dry ingredients and mix lightly until combined. Spoon into cupcake cases and bake them for eight to ten minutes until firm to touch and lightly browned. Serve immediately with some slices of banana and a glass of milk.

Makes 20 mini muffins.

Mini apple muffins
85 g/3 oz plain white flour
1 tsp baking powder
30 g/1 oz rolled oats
55 g/2 oz light muscovado sugar
2 small dessert apples, peeled, cored and diced

1 tbsp sultanas or raisins
25 g/1 oz butter, melted
125 ml/4 oz plain yogurt
1 egg

Preheat the oven to 200°C/400°F/gas mark 6. Line a 12 hole muffin tray with cupcake paper cases. Mix the flour, baking powder, oats and sugar in a bowl. Stir in the chopped apples and sultanas. In another bowl beat together the butter, yogurt and egg. Add this to the dry ingredients and stir quickly and briefly, until just incorporated. Do not over mix. Divide the mixture between the paper cases and bake for about 12 minutes until just firm to touch. Cool on a wire rack.

Makes 12 small muffins.

7 SNACKS

These two recipes make more nutritious alternatives to commercial snacks.

Cheese straws with paprika
110 g/4 oz plain flour
1 tsp ground paprika
55 g/2 oz butter, diced
85 g/3 oz cheddar cheese, grated
1 egg, beaten

Preheat the oven to 200°C/400°F/gas mark 6. Mix the flour, paprika and butter together in a food processor until the mixture resembles breadcrumbs. Stir in the cheese and egg until a soft dough forms. Roll out the dough, on a floured board, to about 1 cm/½ in thick and cut into fingers, or shape into thin rolls. Put on a greased baking sheet and bake for ten minutes. Cool on a wire rack.

Makes 15 straws.

Tortilla crisps
1 large flour tortilla

Preheat the oven to 180°C/350°F/gas mark 4. Cut the tortilla into small wedges. Place the pieces on a baking sheet making sure they are in a single layer. Bake in the oven until golden and crisp – approximately ten minutes, but watch them as it is easy to over cook. Serve as a snack on their own or with a dip.

Makes 4 servings.

END-OF-CHAPTER QUESTIONS

1 *About how much weight do babies gain in their second year?*

2 *Why should babies cut back on milk drinks from 12 months of age?*

3 *What are the four food groups on which a balanced diet is based?*

4 *What is the fifth food group?*

5 *How do you make sure your baby is getting all the nutrients he needs?*

6 *Which vitamins do babies usually not get enough of in their food and therefore need in a vitamin supplement?*

7 *How often should you clean your baby's teeth?*

8 *How much toothpaste should you use for cleaning your baby's teeth?*

9 *Why should you have a feeding regime planned around your baby's sleeps?*

10 *Why should you give both a savoury and sweet course at both main meals?*

7

Weaning and feeding vegetarian babies

In this chapter you will learn:
- *about the different types of vegetarian diets*
- *how to combine foods for a balanced vegetarian diet for your baby.*

Vegetarian diets for babies need a little more care and planning to make sure your baby is having a balanced diet and is getting all the nutrients he needs. If you are from a traditional vegetarian culture then your traditional diet may be adequate. However, if you have emigrated from one country to another you may not always be able to get all the traditional foods you ate in your original homeland. If you have chosen to become vegetarian yourself as an adolescent or adult then the food choices you make for yourself may not necessarily provide your growing and developing baby with all the key nutrients he needs.

Insight

I have seen several mothers who just cut out meat and fish and do not substitute it with any other nutritious alternatives. This can work for them, although some say they have had iron deficiency anaemia themselves. Rapidly growing babies and toddlers will also get iron deficiency anaemia if their vegetarian diet is not well planned.

There are several types of vegetarianism:

- *Semi-vegetarian: only red meat is not eaten.*
- *Piscatarian: meat and poultry are not eaten but fish, milk and eggs are included in the diet.*
- *Lacto-ovo vegetarian: meat, poultry and fish are not eaten but milk and eggs are included.*
- *Lacto-vegetarian: meat, poultry, fish and eggs are not eaten but cows' milk is included.*
- *Vegan: all animal products are excluded – that is, meat, poultry, fish, eggs and cows' milk and products. Soy milk and milk products are usually used in place of cows' milk.*

Babies under six months

Breast milk or an infant formula will be suitable for all vegetarian babies.

VEGAN DIETS

As a vegan mother your breast milk may not contain adequate vitamin B12 for your baby. Your own bones will act as a supply of calcium for your breast milk but unless your diet contains sufficient calcium to replace these losses you might be making yourself prone to osteoporosis in later life. While you are breastfeeding take a vitamin supplement that contains both vitamin D and vitamin B12 and some calcium.

A vegan diet is not recommended for babies as it is unlikely to supply enough nutrients for optimal growth and development. However, if against this advice you choose to bring up your baby as a strict vegan, when you stop breastfeeding the only formula milks not based on cows' milk are soy-based formula milks. These are no longer recommended for babies under six months as there are concerns that the high phyto-oestrogen content may affect the development of babies. If you breastfeed your vegan baby until six months you could change him onto a soy-based formula from then on. The choice in the UK is:

Cow & Gate Infasoy
SMA Wysoy

After you stop breastfeeding continue to give your vegan baby one of these formulas as his milk drink until he is at least two or three years old because they contain more added nutrients than are available in ordinary soya milks.

Other milks such as those based on oats, rice or nuts are not suitable for babies as they don't contain the range of nutrients that babies need from their milk.

Vitamin drops

If you are breastfeeding your baby take a vitamin supplement containing vitamin D yourself, and begin giving your baby vitamin drops from six months. Some mothers have low vitamin D levels during pregnancy which puts their baby at risk of this deficiency also. Mothers most likely to have low vitamin D stores should begin their baby on vitamin drops from birth or one month of age. They are mothers:

▶ *with dark pigmented skins*
▶ *who spend little time outside, e.g. office and shop workers*
▶ *who cover their skin when they are outside*
▶ *who are living in northern areas of the UK.*

Those babies drinking formula milk should begin taking vitamin drops when they are drinking less than 500 ml (17 fl oz) formula milk each day.

Babies over six months

From around six months onwards babies can no longer rely on getting all their nutrients from milk alone. They will need a careful mix of foods to ensure they get all their nutrients. The nutrients that may be low in vegetarian diets are as follows:

Type of vegetarian diet	Nutrients which may be low
Semi-vegetarian: only red meat is not eaten.	Iron
Piscatarian: meat and poultry are not eaten.	Iron
Lacto-ovo vegetarian: meat, poultry and fish are not eaten.	Iron, zinc and omega 3 fats
Lacto-vegetarian: meat, poultry, fish and eggs are not eaten.	Iron, omega 3 fats and vitamin D
Vegan: all animal products are not eaten – that is, meat, poultry, fish, eggs and milk products.	Protein, iron, zinc, calcium and vitamins A, D, K, B2, B12

Making sure a vegetarian diet for babies has adequate nutrients

Changing milk at 12 months: Do not to change to cows' milk at 12 months but continue with a formula milk – either a follow-on formula or a growing-up milk – as these milks are enriched with extra iron, zinc and vitamin D, along with other nutrients.

Protein: Good quality protein containing all the essential amino acids will be provided by meat, fish, eggs, milk and milk products. A combination of nuts or pulses, such as lentils, with a starchy food, such as rice, pasta, potatoes and bread, provides a similar quality of protein. Pulses or nuts or starchy foods on their own do not provide good quality protein as they are all low in one of the essential amino acids. When combined, however, they provide all the essential amino acids.

Iron: Oily fish and dark poultry meat are good sources of iron in the haem form which is readily absorbable (see page 57). Pulses and nuts and starchy foods contain some iron but in the non-haem form. When eaten with fruit or vegetables high in vitamin C it will be better absorbed from these foods. Nuts must be ground for young babies but those over 12 months should manage foods containing chopped nuts. Porridge oats provide some iron for breakfast, but other organic baby cereals are not fortified with iron and provide very little. Non-organic baby cereals are usually fortified with iron, as are some breakfast cereals for children, which are suitable for babies. These can be used for breakfast and offered as snacks. Dried fruit is also a good source of iron and can be added to breakfast cereals or used in milk puddings.

Zinc: By continuing with a formula milk after 12 months extra zinc will be provided as formulas are all fortified with zinc. Wholegrain cereals are a good source of zinc and can be mixed in with white cereals to add extra zinc.

Omega 3 fats: The levels of these in the diet can be boosted by only using oils rich in omega 3 fats: rapeseed oil and walnut oil and to a lesser extent olive and soya oils.

Vitamins A and D will be provided in vitamin drops.

Vegan babies need a more comprehensive vitamin and mineral supplement to provide all the nutrients they need. As babies will all have different likes and dislikes each vegan baby's diet should be assessed by a registered dietician so that a suitable vitamin and mineral supplement can be recommended to provide any nutrients your baby may not be getting enough of. Ask your GP or health visitor for a referral to a registered dietician.

Food combining for vegetarian diets

Make up meals for your vegetarian baby using the same combination of food groups discussed in Chapter 6 – that is, combining foods from the four nutritious food groups. Vegetarian diets can be a bulky diet with more fibre than a non-vegetarian diet and adding in some extra fat will help to make sure there is enough energy. Using fats with a high omega 3 will boost levels of these important fats, particularly in diets where fish is excluded.

Move through the different textures of food and introduce finger foods as described in Chapters 2, 3 and 4. Cut back on milk intake as described in Chapters 4 and 6 so that your baby has plenty of appetite to eat the iron rich foods in food group 4.

The food groups and recommendations are:

Food group	Foods to include	Recommendation
1. Starchy foods: bread, rice, potatoes, pasta and other starchy foods	Bread, chapatti, oat porridge or muesli, breakfast cereals with added iron, rice, couscous, pasta, millet, potatoes, yam, and foods made with flour such as pizza bases, buns, pancakes and scones.	Serve one of these foods at each meal. Choose breakfast cereals that have added iron.
2. Fruit and vegetables	Fresh, frozen, tinned and dried fruits and vegetables. Also pure fruit juices.	Serve fruit at breakfast and at least one vegetable and one fruit at the midday and evening meals.

Food group	Foods to include	Recommendation
	Those high in vitamin C are: ▶ *blackcurrants, kiwi fruit, citrus fruits, tomatoes, peppers and strawberries* ▶ *potato, sweet potatoes and mangoes* ▶ *citrus or blackcurrant fruit juices.* Dried fruit is high in iron.	Always include a fruit or vegetable high in vitamin C at each meal to aid iron absorption.
3. Milk, cheese and yogurt	Breast milk, infant formulas, follow-on milks, growing-up milks, yogurts, cheese, soy-based formula milks, calcium-enriched soya yogurts, tofu.	Before and after 12 months use breast milk or a formula milk as the main milk drink. Serve about three times a day from 12 months onwards.
4. Meat, fish, eggs, nuts and pulses	Poultry, fish, eggs, pulses and foods made from them such as dhal and humous. Use nuts that are ground or chopped.	Serve at each meal.
Foods high in fat	Cream, butter, margarines and mayonnaise. Oils high in omega 3 fats are rapeseed oil and walnut oil. Oils with a good balance of omega 3 and 6 fats are olive oil and soya oil.	Use in cooking and add to boost energy content of foods.

(Contd)

Food group	Foods to include	Recommendation
Foods high in sugar	Jam, honey, syrup, confectionery.	Use occasionally for babies over 12 months.
Foods high in fat and sugar	Ice cream, biscuits, cakes, chocolate.	Use occasionally for babies over 12 months.

Recommendations and menu plans for each type of vegetarian food pattern

1 SEMI-VEGETARIAN: ONLY RED MEAT IS NOT EATEN

Offer poultry, oily fish, fish, eggs and pulses.

When you serve poultry give your baby dark poultry meat such as legs and thighs as this has a higher iron content than light meat such as that on the breast of a chicken or turkey.

Combine eggs, pulses or nuts with a high vitamin C food when you use these rather than with poultry or fish.

Sample menu plan:

	Day 1	Day 2	Day 3
Breakfast	Baby cereal with added iron. Banana slices. Small glass diluted orange juice.	Breakfast cereal with added iron. Cooked apple. Small glass diluted orange juice.	Baby muesli with added ground almonds and strawberries.

	Day 1	*Day 2*	*Day 3*
Midday meal	Chicken curry and rice. Broccoli. Yogurt and strawberries.	Salmon and potato fish cakes. Cauliflower and carrot. Rice pudding and mango slices.	Pasta with minced turkey in bolognaise sauce. Green beans. Egg custard and fresh peaches.
Evening meal	Poached fish. Mashed sweet potato and spinach. Raspberries.	Scrambled egg with toast fingers. Pepper slices and courgette sticks. Pear slices.	Pitta bread with humous. Carrot and cucumber sticks. Kiwi slices.

2 PISCATARIAN: MEAT AND POULTRY ARE NOT EATEN

Use fish frequently and use oily fish up to about four times per week.

Offer one of the following at each of the three meals:

▶ *fish*
▶ *oily fish*
▶ *egg, nuts or pulses combined with a high vitamin C food.*

Sample menu plan:

	Day 1	*Day 2*	*Day 3*
Breakfast	Baby cereal with added iron. Banana slices. Small glass diluted orange juice.	Breakfast cereal with added iron. Cooked apple. Small glass diluted orange juice.	Baby muesli with added ground almonds and strawberries.

(Contd)

	Day 1	Day 2	Day 3
Midday meal	Chickpea curry with courgette and cauliflower. Rice. Yogurt and strawberries.	Salmon and potato fish cakes. Broccoli and carrot. Rice pudding and mango slices.	Pasta with lentils in bolognaise sauce. Green beans. Egg custard and fresh peaches.
Evening meal	Poached fish. Mashed sweet potato and spinach. Raspberries.	Scrambled egg with toast fingers. Pepper slices and courgette sticks. Pear slices.	Pitta bread with humous. Carrot and cucumber sticks. Kiwi slices.

3 *LACTO-OVO VEGETARIAN: MEAT, POULTRY AND FISH ARE NOT EATEN*

At each meal offer:

- ▶ *egg, nuts or pulses combined with a high vitamin C food*
- ▶ *a cereal food.*

To increase the omega 3 fats in the diet:

- ▶ *use rapeseed oil for cooking*
- ▶ *use walnut oil or olive oil for dressings*
- ▶ *use ground walnuts sprinkled on breakfast cereal, fruit or mixed into puddings.*

Sample menu plan:

	Day 1	*Day 2*	*Day 3*
Breakfast	Baby cereal with added iron. Banana slices. Small glass diluted orange juice.	Breakfast cereal with added iron. Cooked apple. Small glass diluted orange juice.	Baby muesli with added ground walnuts and strawberries.
Midday meal	Chickpea curry with courgette and cauliflower. Rice. Yogurt and strawberries.	Dhal and rice. Broccoli and carrot. Rice pudding and mango slices.	Pasta with lentils in bolognaise sauce. Green beans. Egg custard and fresh peaches.
Evening meal	Tofu stir-fry with noodles and spinach. Raspberries.	Scrambled egg with toast fingers. Pepper slices and courgette sticks. Pear slices.	Pitta bread with humous. Carrot and cucumber sticks. Kiwi slices.

4 LACTO-VEGETARIAN: MEAT, POULTRY, FISH AND EGGS ARE NOT EATEN

At each meal offer:

▶ *nuts or pulses combined with a high vitamin C food*
▶ *a cereal food.*

To increase the omega 3 fats in the diet:

▶ *use rapeseed oil for cooking*
▶ *use walnut oil or olive oil for dressings*

▶ *use ground walnuts sprinkled on breakfast cereal, fruit or mixed into puddings.*

Sample menu plan:

	Day 1	Day 2	Day 3
Breakfast	Baby cereal with added iron. Banana slices. Small glass diluted orange juice.	Breakfast cereal with added iron. Cooked apple. Small glass diluted orange juice.	Baby muesli with added ground walnuts and strawberries.
Midday meal	Chickpea curry with courgette and cauliflower. Rice. Yogurt and strawberries.	Dhal and rice. Broccoli and carrot. Rice pudding and mango slices.	Pasta with lentils in bolognaise sauce. Green beans. Egg custard and fresh peaches.
Evening meal	Tofu stir-fry with noodles and spinach. Raspberries.	Toast fingers with peanut butter. Pepper slices and courgette sticks. Pear slices.	Pitta bread with humous. Carrot and cucumber sticks. Kiwi slices.

5 VEGAN: ALL ANIMAL PRODUCTS ARE NOT EATEN – THAT IS, MEAT, POULTRY, FISH, EGGS AND MILK PRODUCTS

A vegan diet is very restricted and is not usually recommended because babies obtain many nutrients from their milk. If you do wish to embark on a vegan diet, breastfeed your baby or use a soya-based formula milk until he is at least two years old. Ask to see a registered dietician to get some individualized advice on how suitable your family foods are for weaning your baby. A dietician will also be able to recommend a suitable vitamin and mineral supplement.

At each meal you need to combine foods to make sure your baby is having good quality protein and some high-iron foods at each meal along with a food rich in vitamin C.

At each meal offer a combination of:

▶ *a cereal-based food*
▶ *nuts or pulses*
▶ *a food high in vitamin C.*

6 *MORE RESTRICTED DIETS*

Diets with more restrictions than a vegan diet are unsuitable for babies and older children. Babies on macrobiotic and fruitarian diets have become severely malnourished with deficiencies of various nutrients. There have been cases of parents who have refused to provide their babies with a more nutritious diet, recommended by healthcare professionals. These parents' babies and children have been taken into care to prevent ill health and death from malnutrition.

Vegetarian recipes

Recipes with poultry, fish, eggs and milk are included in the other chapters. The recipes below are based on pulses including lentils, chickpeas, and other starchy beans.

Choose puddings that include dried fruit or nuts to provide some extra iron for your vegetarian baby.

Cooked and mashed lentils, puréed chickpeas or mashed tofu can be added to any combination of vegetables. Lentils are more usually cooked with spices and ghee as dhal.

Cooking red lentils
Wash the lentils and rinse well. Place in a pan and cover with cold water and bring to the boil. Turn the heat down and simmer for about 15 minutes until soft.

Red lentil dhal
3 tbsp split red lentils
250 ml/8 fl oz water
2 small spring onions, very finely chopped
1 garlic clove, peeled and finely chopped
½ tbsp melted ghee or rapeseed oil
¼ tsp ground turmeric
¼ tsp ground cumin

Thoroughly wash, drain and place the lentils in a small saucepan with the water and bring to the boil. Simmer uncovered for ten minutes, stirring frequently and removing any scum that forms. Cover and cook for a further 30 minutes or so, stirring occasionally until the lentils are soft and form a moist 'porridge'. In a separate pan gently heat the ghee or rapeseed oil, add the onion and fry until nicely browned. Add the garlic and fry for a further two or three minutes. Next add the ground spices and fry for a further two minutes. Finally, add the contents of the pan to the lentils and stir to fully combine for two minutes. If the dhal is too thick, add further water; if too thin, simmer gently until reduced.

Cooking green puy lentils
Wash the lentils and rinse well. Place in a pan and cover with cold water and bring to the boil. Boil rapidly for ten minutes, then reduce the heat and simmer for 30–40 minutes or until tender. Drain.

Cooking chickpeas

Canned precooked chickpeas are readily available in most stores but, if you prefer, you can buy dried chickpeas and cook them yourself.

Cover the chickpeas with cold water and leave them to soak overnight. Drain and rinse them with fresh water. Add fresh water until the chickpeas are covered in water again and bring to the boil. Reduce the heat and simmer gently until chickpeas are soft (about one hour).

Lentils with carrot and coriander

3 tbsp red lentils
½ medium potato (about 60 g/2 oz), peeled and diced
1 small carrot (about 60 g/2 oz), peeled and diced
¼ tsp ground coriander
½ tsp tomato purée, squeezed
150 ml/¼ pint water

Rinse the lentils thoroughly with water by putting them in a sieve and immersing in a bowl of water. Remove them from the water and drain. Put the lentils, diced vegetables, water and coriander in a pan and cover with a tight-fitting lid. Bring to the boil and simmer gently for about 20 minutes until the vegetables are tender and the lentils are soft. Add the tomato purée and mix together in a blender until smooth. If the purée is too thick add some cooled, boiled water to thin down.

Makes 6–8 servings.

Chickpeas, sweet potato and cauliflower mash

1 small sweet potato, peeled and diced
6 small cauliflower florets
4 tbsp cooked chickpeas
½ tsp ground cumin

Put water in a small saucepan and bring to the boil. Add the sweet potato pieces and pop the cauliflower florets on top. Cover with a tight-fitting lid and bring back to the boil. Simmer gently for about ten minutes until both vegetables are tender. Check to make sure the water does not boil away, add a little more if necessary. Mash the vegetables. Purée the chickpeas with the cumin and stir into the mashed vegetables.

Makes 6 servings.

Humous
400 g/14 oz can chickpeas, drained and rinsed
3 tbsp olive oil
juice of 1 lemon
½ tsp cumin
1 clove garlic, crushed

Put all the ingredients into bowl and purée with a handheld blender.

Stir humous into any combination of vegetables.

Creamed tofu and parsnip
Tofu is an excellent source of vegetarian protein. The vitamin C in the potatoes and orange juice boost the absorption of iron from the tofu.

1 small parsnip (60 g/2 oz), peeled and diced
1 small potato (60 g/2 oz), peeled and diced
1 small carrot (60 g/2 oz), peeled and diced
75 g/3 oz tofu, drained and crumbled
juice of ½ orange

Cook the diced potatoes, parsnips and carrots together by steaming or adding to about 100 ml/3½ fl oz boiling water and simmering gently. Either method takes about ten minutes. Purée the cooked vegetables, tofu and orange juice together. Mix until smooth, adding in some baby milk if necessary.

Makes 4–6 servings.

Spinach dhal
The vitamin C in the pepper and tomatoes will boost iron absorption from the lentils and spinach.

55 g/2 oz red lentils, rinsed and drained
30 g/2 tbsp basmati or long grain rice, rinsed and drained
1 tsp olive oil
½ red pepper, cored, deseeded and sliced
pinch ground cumin
pinch ground coriander
250 ml/8 fl oz water
30 g/1 oz spinach, washed thoroughly and chopped
3 tbsp chopped tomatoes

Put the lentils, rice, chopped red pepper, oil, spices and water in a saucepan and bring to the boil. Cover and simmer until rice is tender (about 25 minutes).

Stir in the spinach and tomatoes and cook for a further two or three minutes, until the spinach has wilted and it is hot right through. Mash with a fork.

Makes 3–4 servings.

2 SAVOURY COURSES FROM NINE MONTHS

Courgette, cauliflower and chickpea curry
This is a mild and creamy, first curry to introduce your baby to the taste if you enjoy curries as family food. The vegetarian protein comes from chickpeas and peanut butter. The tomato purée contains vitamin C and boosts iron absorption.

1 tbsp rapeseed oil
1 small onion, finely chopped
2 tsp mild curry paste
1 tbsp tomato purée

2 tbsp smooth peanut butter (optional)
250 ml/8 fl oz vegetable stock or water
½ medium cauliflower, cut into florets
2 medium courgettes, cubed
400 g/14 oz can chickpeas, drained
250 ml/8 fl oz natural bio-yogurt

Fry the onion in the oil over a gentle heat until softened. Add the
cauliflower and courgettes and cook for a further two minutes.
Now stir in the curry paste, tomato purée, peanut butter, chickpeas
and vegetable stock or water. Cover and simmer for 20 minutes.
Remove from the heat and allow to stand for ten minutes before
stirring in the yogurt. Take out a portion and mash (for those six
to nine month babies) or cut up (for those over nine months).
Serve with rice and sliced bananas.

Makes 6–10 portions.

Pasta with lentil bolognaise sauce
3 tbsp puy lentils, rinsed
½ tbsp olive oil
2 spring onions, finely sliced
1 small clove garlic
½ small courgette, diced
2 small button mushrooms, washed and diced
2 tbsp chopped tomatoes
1 tsp tomato purée
½ tsp dried mixed herbs
pinch black pepper
55 g/2 oz pasta spirals

Put the lentils into a saucepan and add water to cover them.
Bring to the boil and simmer until the lentils are tender (about
25 minutes). Meanwhile, heat the oil in a pan and add the onion,
garlic, courgette and mushrooms. Stir-fry for five to ten minutes,
until tender. Add the chopped tomatoes, tomato pureé, herbs
and pepper. Cover and cook gently for about five minutes. Drain
the cooked lentils and stir into the vegetable sauce. Cook pasta

according to the instructions on the packet. Drain well. Keep a few pasta spirals as finger foods and mash the rest of the pasta into the lentil sauce. Serve sprinkled with grated cheese.

Makes 2–3 servings.

Tofu and avocado spread
½ ripe avocado, stone and skin removed
55 g/2 oz tofu, broken into pieces
juice of ½ lemon
1 small clove garlic
½ tbsp fresh parsley
1 tsp olive oil

Put all the ingredients in a bowl and purée with a hand blender until the mixture is smooth. Spoon into a bowl and garnish with a slice of lemon. Store in the fridge, tightly covered with cling film.

Makes 4–6 servings.

3 SAVOURY COURSES FROM 12 MONTHS

Butternut squash and chickpea risotto
2 litres/3½ pints vegetable stock
2 cloves garlic, peeled
large pinch saffron strands
2 tbsp tomato purée
1 small butternut squash, peeled, deseeded and cut into small cubes
2 tbsp butter
1 small onion, peeled and chopped
450 g/1 lb risotto rice
400 g/14 oz can chickpeas, drained
2 tbsp chopped parsley
55 g/2 oz grated parmesan cheese

In a pan place the stock, garlic, saffron, tomato purée and butternut squash cubes. Simmer for 10–15 minutes until the squash is just tender. Using a slotted spoon transfer the squash to a plate and set aside. Remove the garlic cloves and discard. Melt the butter in a heavy-based pan, add the onion and sauté for a few minutes until soft. Add the rice, stir well and continue to cook gently over a low heat for a minute or two. Gradually add the stock a ladle at a time. Stir constantly, gradually adding more liquid as the rice absorbs it. When the rice is just tender add the squash and the chickpeas. Keep adding stock and stirring until the rice is creamy and all the stock is absorbed. When cooked, stir in the cheese and sprinkle with chopped parsley. Serve with a green vegetable.

Makes 6–8 servings.

Mini falafel
400 g/14 oz can chickpeas, rinsed and drained
1 small onion, finely chopped
1 clove garlic, peeled and finely chopped
1 tbsp fresh coriander leaves, washed and chopped
1 tsp ground coriander
1 tsp ground cumin
½ tsp ground turmeric
2–4 tbsp flour
1–2 tbsp olive oil

Place the chickpeas in a food processor with the onion, garlic, cumin, turmeric and both types of coriander. Process until you have a smooth purée. Let the mixture rest for at least 30 minutes. Take walnut-sized portions and shape each into a small, flat, round shape 1 cm/½ inch thick. Roll them lightly in the flour and chill for another 30 minutes. Heat the oil in a frying pan and cook the falafel over a gentle medium heat for about ten minutes, turning frequently.

Makes 4–6 servings.

Spicy cannellini beans with mushrooms
2 tbsp olive oil
2 medium onions, sliced
1 tsp ground cumin

1 tsp ground coriander
1 tsp ground turmeric
½ tsp ground cinnamon
220 g/8 oz mushrooms, chopped
1 red pepper, deseeded and sliced
400 g/14 oz tin cannellini beans, drained
400 g/14 oz chopped tomatoes
1 tsp tomato purée
pinch black pepper
2 tbsp fresh coriander leaves or parsley, chopped

Heat the oil in a large non-stick frying pan and cook the onions until transparent and soft. Add all the spices and stir for a minute then add the mushrooms and pepper. Cook for another minute or so, then add the beans, tomatoes, tomato purée and black pepper. Cover and simmer for 15 minutes. Sprinkle with coriander or parsley before serving. Serve with pasta or rice and a green vegetable.

Makes 4–6 servings.

Tofu stir-fry
1 tbsp yellow bean sauce
1 tbsp smooth peanut butter
juice of 1 lemon
1 tbsp olive oil
1 tsp grated fresh ginger
pinch mild chilli powder
1 clove garlic, peeled and crushed
115 g/4 oz firm tofu, drained and sliced
1 courgette, diced
1 orange pepper, deseeded and diced
85 g/3 oz fresh bean sprouts

In a bowl, mix together the yellow bean sauce, peanut butter and lemon juice. Heat the oil in a non-stick frying pan and stir- fry the ginger, chilli and garlic for a minute. Add the tofu slices and fry for a minute turning once. Add the courgette, orange pepper and

bean sprouts and continue stir-frying for two to three minutes.
Add the sauce mixture and stir-fry for one to two minutes until
well combined. Serve with noodles or rice.

Makes 2–4 servings.

4 PUDDINGS

Rhubarb crumble
55 g/2 oz plain flour
45 g/1½ oz butter, cut into small cubes
30 g/1 oz rolled oats
3 tbsp ground almonds
45 g/1½ oz soft dark brown sugar
450 g/1 lb rhubarb
2 tbsp sugar

Preheat the oven to 180°C/350°F/gas mark 4. To make the crumble
topping, put the flour, oats and butter into a food processor and
process until the mixture resembles coarse crumbs. Stir in the
ground almonds and brown sugar. Prepare the rhubarb by cutting
into chunks and cooking in a little water with the 2 tbsp sugar
until beginning to soften. Put the rhubarb in a small ovenproof
dish. Sprinkle the crumble on top and bake in the oven for 30–40
minutes, until the top is lightly browned. Serve with ice cream or
custard.

Makes 4–6 servings.

Date and walnut loaf
The fruit and nuts make this sweet, moist cake a nutritious snack.
Walnuts are high in essential fatty acids. If it isn't eaten all at once
this will keep well, in fact it becomes more moist when stored for a
day or two.

110 g/4 oz soft butter or margarine
175 g/6 oz soft brown sugar
2 eggs

110 g/4 oz wholemeal flour
110 g/4 oz plain white flour
1½ tsp baking powder
110 g/4 oz walnuts, finely chopped
110 g/4 oz pitted dates, chopped
3–4 tbsp water

Preheat the oven to 180°C/350°F/gas mark 4. Grease a loaf tin.
Put the butter, sugar, eggs, flour and baking powder in a food
processor. Process for a few seconds until mixed. Add the walnuts,
dates and water. Mix for another few seconds but do not over
process. Turn the mixture into the loaf tin spreading it out evenly.
Bake for one hour until the loaf feels springy. To test if it is ready
insert a fine skewer and then remove. The skewer should come out
clean. Allow to cool in the tin for a few minutes before turning out.
Serve warm or cold. To store, wrap in foil.

Makes 8–10 slices.

Warm fruit salad
55 g/2 oz dried peaches or pears
55 g/2 oz dried apple rings
40 g/1½ oz dried apricots
40 g/1½ oz sultanas
100 ml/3½ fl oz orange juice
100 ml/3½ fl oz water
1 clove
1 cinnamon stick

Place all the ingredients in a pan and bring to the boil. Cover and
simmer until all the fruits are tender (about ten minutes). Remove
the clove and cinnamon and allow to cool. Chill until required.
Serve with yogurt, custard or ice cream.

Makes 4–6 portions.

END-OF-CHAPTER QUESTIONS

1 Which nutrients are most likely to be low in a vegetarian diet?

2 Which nutrients are likely to be low in a vegan diet?

3 Why is a vegan diet not recommended for babies?

4 A combination of which types of foods provides a similar quality of protein to that found in meat, fish, eggs and meat?

5 When can a vegetarian baby change to cows' milk?

6 Which foods provide the best source of omega 3 fats for babies that do not eat fish?

8

Fussy eating and food refusal in the second year

In this chapter you will learn:
- *why babies become fussy eaters in their second year*
- *why babies refuse to eat*
- *how food battles develop*
- *how you can help to resolve your baby's fussy, faddy eating.*

Sometime during his second year you will begin to notice your baby is asserting his independence about what he will eat and what he won't eat. It may be most noticeable around the time he is about 18 months old but can be any time in this second year. Your baby may:

▶ *eat less than you expect him to*
▶ *refuse to taste new foods you offer*
▶ *refuse to eat foods he has eaten before*
▶ *refuse to eat a whole meal.*

There are many reasons why babies refuse foods or even a whole meal and most parents worry unnecessarily about this.

Why most young toddlers are fussy eaters

Young toddlers become fussy because they are going through a normal stage in their development where they become wary of trying new foods. It is called a neophobic response to food because neophobia means fear of new.

This stage of food neophobia develops soon after babies have begun walking and are becoming more adept at getting about and can roam further to investigate their environment. The fear of new foods is probably a survival mechanism to prevent the mobile young toddlers from harming themselves through eating anything and everything. If they were to taste any interesting looking berry on a bush they could well poison themselves.

As was emphasized in Chapters 3 and 4, between six and twelve months of age, most babies are willing to try many different foods, flavours and textures. By about 12 months of age babies already have ideas about what foods they like, and what those foods look like. Once the neophobic stage begins, young toddlers may reject a food on sight without wanting to try it. Toddlers may also reject foods that look slightly different from those that they usually eat, for example, a different type of bread or a yogurt in a different carton.

Insight
This stage comes as a shock to mothers of babies who have previously eaten well. It is very exasperating because a baby is not able to tell you why he doesn't want to even try the food.

How common is fussy eating?

As it is a specific stage of development, all young mobile toddlers will go through it, however, it will be more evident in some toddlers than others. If your baby is happily eating the wide range of most of your family foods by the time he is beginning his second year of life then you may not be offering many foods that he is not familiar with and you may not notice this stage. It will be more evident in babies who have only been offered a narrow range of foods before this neophobic phase begins. These young toddlers may restrict themselves to a very small range of foods and their parents often become quite exasperated and worry that their baby is not eating enough and not getting enough nutrients to grow and develop.

FUSSY EATING NORMALLY RESOLVES WITH TIME

Over time, and in a supportive environment, almost all babies will eventually grow out of this neophobic phase. Babies learn by copying their parents, siblings and peers. When eating with you and others your baby will notice which foods you are eating and he will learn that these foods are safe to eat. With time and seeing you eating them a few times he will become confident to taste those foods. However, he may need to taste them several times to reassure himself that he likes them. Some babies may need to be offered a new food ten or more times before they learn to like it.

By the same learning process if he sees a sibling or parent rejecting a food he may also reject that food. You need to eat with your baby as often as possible, eat the foods you want him to eat and make positive comments about the food.

To help him through this stage just encouraging him to taste the new food is enough; he does not need to eat a lot of it. If he will not even try the new food, then wait and offer it again when you are next eating it.

Insight

When I tell parents their baby will eventually grow out of this phase they find it reassuring, but each time a baby refuses the food that has been prepared there is a sense of disappointment for the parent who has prepared the food. Day to day over a long time this can be quite depressing – especially for a mother who prides herself on her cooking.

Other reasons for food refusal

Not all food refusal will be due to this phase of food neophobia. Young toddlers may also be reluctant to eat well for other reasons.

As he will not be able to explain to you why he doesn't want to eat, it will be up to you to determine the reason yourself.

However, he will signal to you quite clearly when he has eaten enough and does not want any more.

Ways of refusing food
Your baby is saying he does not want more food when he:

▶ *says no*
▶ *keeps his mouth shut when food is offered*
▶ *turns his head away from the food being offered*
▶ *puts his hand in front of his mouth*
▶ *pushes away a spoon, bowl or plate containing food*
▶ *holds food in his mouth and refuses to swallow it*
▶ *spits food out repeatedly*
▶ *cries, shouts or screams*
▶ *tries to climb out of the highchair*
▶ *gags or retches.*

Insight
I found these signs difficult to accept when I had especially prepared a meal and very little was eaten. There was a strong temptation to ignore these signs and carry on offering the food. However, there was very little point as we both just got frustrated.

He could be telling you he has had enough because:

▶ *He is no longer hungry – he has eaten enough to satisfy his hunger. A common mistake parents make is to believe that they know better than their baby how much he should eat. A parent may have in their mind a set quantity. It may be the contents of the jar they have opened or the quantity of food they have lovingly prepared. It may even be an educated guess based on roughly the quantities eaten over the previous few days. However, babies' appetites vary widely from day to day*

*and on how they are feeling at the time. They will also vary
because they grow in spurts so their calorie needs vary from
time to time.*

▶ *He may be bored of eating that course and ready to eat
something different. Always offer two courses: a savoury
course followed by a pudding. It gives two chances for
calories and nutrients to be taken in. Make sure puddings
are nutritious, based on some fruit and containing other
ingredients such as flour, milk and/or eggs.*

▶ *He doesn't like that food. Babies' taste buds are very sensitive
and change with time. You may be offering a food that he
is prepared to taste a little of but he has not yet had enough
tastes to like the food enough to enjoy a large quantity of it.
Alternatively, it may be a taste he just doesn't like. Babies
have their own preferences. Some prefer foods that are not all
mashed together so that they can choose to eat more of one
and less of another.*

▶ *He may have become bored because he is not involved in
the meal. Give him his own spoon so that he can feed himself
and include finger foods with every meal.*

▶ *He may have become bored with a food if you have been
offering it very frequently. Often babies enjoy one particular
food and then, just when you have bought a large stock,
decide they want a break from that particular food.*

▶ *He is not hungry at mealtimes because there is no set meal
pattern and he grazes on food between meals.*

▶ *He is not hungry for food because he takes a lot of calories
from drinks such as too much milk or large volumes of juices
and squashes. Some babies have a tendency to do this as they
find drinking easier than the effort involved in eating. If this
is the problem you will need to cut back on fluid – see later in
this chapter. Make sure there is a set meal and snack routine
so that he is not eating or drinking too close to a mealtime.*

▶ *He is not hungry for food because he is still waking and
drinking milk during the night.*

▶ *He is distracted by toys, games, TV or a new environment.
Young toddlers can only concentrate on one thing at a time
and if something else distracts him he will stop eating. If you*

are out he may be more curious about his new environment or the people there than the meal. One lost meal won't matter – he will probably eat more at the next meal that you offer on familiar ground.

▶ *He is too tired to eat. Young toddlers, like babies, enjoy a routine and regular mealtimes. However, life does not always go to plan. In general try and avoid meals too close to bedtime or their daytime sleep. When this is unavoidable make that meal more a quick snack and a drink of milk and give the meal later when he has had a sleep and is wide awake and alert. After a very busy time or a day full of new experiences he may be just too exhausted to eat well.*

▶ *He is too grumpy because he has become over-hungry. Babies do not realize why they are grumpy and if he has gone too long since his last meal he will just know he is grumpy and will not realize that by eating he will begin to feel better. This is why it is so important to have a set routine of meals.*

▶ *He is feeling unwell – babies may refuse food if they have a sore throat, are getting a cold or are fighting an infection but don't yet have the symptoms of a temperature or runny nose for you to notice. Appetite is often reduced when a child has a temperature. Painful gums during teething will also reduce his appetite. You will know the feeling of not being hungry a day or so before getting a heavy cold or flu – just remember your baby is not able to explain this to you. If you insist he tries to eat, you will be making him more miserable and may put him off the food you are attempting to feed as an association with that food and feeling miserable may be set up.*

▶ *He is constipated. This may have developed because of poor eating and drinking but there may also be a physical reason why he is constipated. You will probably be aware that your baby is constipated because he will strain a lot when passing a stool and may also cry with the pain. Constipation reduces appetite and coercing a constipated baby to eat more will be a lost cause. Check the amount of fluid your baby is drinking – inadequate fluid is a cause of constipation. Inadequate fibre is also a cause of constipation but it will be difficult to encourage your baby to eat more of any food including high-fibre foods*

while he has constipation. Ask your doctor to treat the
constipation first and when it has resolved make sure you offer
your baby six to eight drinks of 100–120 ml/3½–4 fl oz per
day and offer a fibre-containing food at each meal. Fibre-
containing foods are fruit and vegetables, pulses and cereals.

▶ *He has iron deficiency anaemia – young toddlers who are not*
eating enough iron rich foods and become anaemic will have
a reduced appetite. You may also notice they are tired and
miserable and pick up colds and other infections frequently.
To test for anaemia your baby will need to have a blood test
which you GP can arrange. To treat the anaemia he will be
given an iron supplement. As he gets better make sure you are
offering iron rich foods at each meal (see pages 57 and 215).

▶ *He has reflux – although this is fairly common in babies, most*
have grown out of it by about one year old. However, in some
babies it may persist longer but without seeing any posseting
you may be unaware that food and stomach acid are still
coming back up the oesophagus and causing discomfort or pain
when your baby is eating. Mealtimes will become unpleasant
times for him which will reduce his appetite. If you suspect this
is happening then there are simple tests which can be done at a
hospital to check this. Your GP can arrange a referral for you.

▶ *He is anxious at mealtimes. This may be because he has had*
negative experiences at mealtimes. The negative experience
may involve him having been force-fed or pressured to eat
something he didn't like or was scared of. Alternatively, the
negative experiences may involve others if there is a lot of
tension, shouting or arguing at mealtimes. Whatever the cause
of his unhappiness, if he is becoming anxious as mealtimes
approach, he will lose his appetite.

Reasons for poor eating
Babies do not eat well if they are:

▶ *not hungry*
▶ *tired*
▶ *distracted by toys, games, TV, a new environment*

(Contd)

> ▶ *anxious, sad, lonely or insecure*
> ▶ *feeling grumpy or unwell*
> ▶ *constipated*
> ▶ *anaemic*
>
> and if:
>
> ▶ *there isn't a routine to mealtimes*
> ▶ *the experience around mealtimes is negative*
> ▶ *they have a medical problem such as gastro-oesophageal reflux.*

Insight

When parents tell me that their baby refuses even to get into the highchair this tells me that their baby feels under pressure at mealtimes and does not enjoy the mealtime experience.

How do food battles between babies and parents develop?

There are several ways food battles can begin and most will involve an anxious parent and a combination of the following factors:

Over-estimating how much food your baby needs

You may expect your baby to eat more than he needs. If you are anxious that he is not eating enough you may begin to coerce him to eat more. You may even begin to trick him into opening his mouth so you can pop some more food in. You may also try to reward him for eating food that he does not want or need. As a last resort, some parents resort to force-feeding. Force-feeding at mealtimes will make a baby anxious and frightened around food. It can mean that he will lose his appetite before he even starts the meal. Often meals are extended so long that your baby becomes bored. Most babies eat whatever food they are going to eat in the first 20 minutes of the meal.

Parents may over-estimate how much food their baby needs because they have noticed he is eating less than another baby of a similar age or even younger. However, babies can regulate their appetite to meet their growth needs. This means that babies will be hungry only for the amount of food that they need to eat. They are better at knowing how much they need to eat than their parents. Babies' appetites can also change from day to day. If a baby is growing normally then he is eating as much as he needs.

Parents usually end up losing when they try to make their baby eat more than he needs or wants; you invest time and effort with little return and your baby can become miserable, bored and upset. If this pattern occurs repeatedly, he will become anxious as each meal begins, and this will reduce his appetite.

Giving him more attention when he doesn't eat

Your baby naturally loves your attention. If you are giving him more attention when he doesn't eat than when he does, he may refuse to eat to get your attention. To him the attention of a cross parent is better than no attention.

A parent who is unhappy or even depressed may not interact with their baby as much as their baby would like. If he finds the only way to elicit a response from you is to refuse to eat then he will do this.

He wants to assert himself

Babies of one to two years old increasingly want to assert themselves. They often say no to requests and enjoy doing so.

Parents tend to become more anxious when a baby refuses food than when he won't wear a hat or socks, but to the baby it is all just part of the same game.

Not allowing him to be involved in the meal

He may want to be more involved in the meal than you are allowing him to be. Anxious parents often want to control the meal so prefer to do all the spoon-feeding themselves. However, babies need to be allowed to try feeding themselves and to make a mess. They need to learn about food and playing with it helps them learn.

EXACERBATING THE FOOD BATTLE

Once meals have become stressful a baby will become anxious as mealtimes approach and lose his appetite, thus reducing further the quantity he then eats. This can make a parent more anxious and more determined to make their baby eat. Parents may resort to:

▶ *chasing their baby around the room with a spoon of food*
▶ *playing games and tricking him into opening his mouth and then popping some food in*
▶ *pleading with him to eat more*
▶ *offering him rewards if he will eat more.*

Why are some parents anxious about food?

There are valid reasons why some parents may become over-anxious about the quantity of food and type of food their baby eats:

▶ *If your baby was born prematurely and his survival was in doubt then you may have become very anxious about everything including how much food he eats.*
▶ *If your baby had a hospital admission soon after birth for dehydration then you may continue to feel anxious about not being able to feed your baby properly.*
▶ *A healthcare professional may have implied that your baby had not gained enough weight and you felt that you were not feeding him adequately.*
▶ *Your baby may be smaller than another baby of the same age or younger.*

It may be difficult to stop feeling anxious but if you understand why you feel anxious you may be able to manage those anxious feelings and put them into perspective.

Overcoming anxieties around your baby's food intake

Babies don't need to eat well at every meal, every day.

The amount of each nutrient needed to keep them healthy is an average amount. Most nutrients are stored in the body and these stores will last them some time. If he doesn't have milk one day his bones will not crack up. Be satisfied that over a period of two weeks or so, by eating more on some days and less on other days he will be getting on average what he needs.

Make sure each meal and snack is nutritious so that when he does eat well he is getting plenty of nutrients.

Plan out the feeding regime for your baby around his usual sleeps and you will probably find he never goes longer than three hours awake without being offered some food. When this is the case you can feel confident that if he refuses to eat at one meal or snack it won't be long until he is next offered food.

Follow this advice:

▶ *Offer your baby food regularly: three meals and two to three planned snacks each day.*
▶ *Leave about two and a half to three hours between each meal and snack.*
▶ *Let him eat as much as he wishes.*
▶ *When he indicates he has had enough ask him once or twice if he would like some more.*
▶ *If he indicates again that he has had enough, take the food away and say something positive like: 'Good boy, you have eaten some potato'.*
▶ *Don't coerce him to eat more.*
▶ *Don't look anxious.*
▶ *Don't make any negative comments.*
▶ *Offer him a second course and repeat as above.*

However difficult this seems, when he eats very little you can be confident that you will be offering him food again in another two and a half to three hours. He can eat more then if he is hungry.

Keep an open mind about the quantity your baby needs. Respect his decision when he indicates to you that he has had enough and honour it. In the long term it is important that children learn to know when they are full and no longer hungry. Some obese children have no idea when they feel satiated and consequently eat larger quantities of food than they need.

Accept that his height is normal for him. Height is largely determined by his genes and height is much less affected by his food intake than is weight. If he is not eating enough he may lose a little weight but he will soon regain this weight when he is eating better.

Ask your health visitor or GP to check for any underlying medical reasons why he would not be eating enough. If there are no reasons, then have confidence that he knows better than you do about how much he needs to eat.

During mealtimes also try to remember:

- *Be positive. Always try to make each mealtime enjoyable for you both. It is up to you to teach your children that eating is one of life's great pleasures and not something to be endured.*
- *Smile encouragement whenever you offer food. This is especially important if you are offering something new or a food you don't like yourself and you are concerned your child might not like it as well. If you don't smile to conceal your concern your child will pick up your anxiety and may be averse to trying the food.*
- *Don't allow meals to go on for too long.*
- *Remember babies learn by copying, so eat with your baby as often as possible. Show him that you find eating fun and pleasurable.*
- *Don't use foods to bribe with. If you offer Food B as a reward for eating up Food A then in essence you are telling him that*

Food B is a desirable food and Food A is not desirable – usually the opposite to the health message you have in your mind.

▶ *Allow your baby to feed himself and to make a mess. Offer him some finger foods at every meal.*

▶ *Accept that he may take some time to be confident enough to try a new food and will only take tiny tastes of it to begin with. He needs time to learn to like new tastes.*

▶ *If one meal turns into a disaster, don't feel guilty. Put it behind you and approach the next meal positively. Parents also learn by making mistakes. I fell into some of these traps myself when my children were babies. Nobody should expect to be a perfect parent.*

Insight

I think that smiling and making all meals a really pleasant experience is the most important but perhaps the hardest thing to do consistently.

Checklist of dos and don'ts

Do	Reason
1 Eat with your baby as often as possible.	Babies learn by copying their parents and other children.
2 Develop a daily routine of three meals and two to three snacks around his sleeping pattern.	Babies don't eat well if they become over-hungry or very tired.
3 Check he is not still drinking too much milk – no large bottles of milk and no more than three small cups of 120 ml/4 fl oz each day once over 12 months.	Too much milk will fill him up and leave him little appetite for food.

(Contd)

Do	Reason
4 Check he is not drinking large quantities of fruit juice or other sweet drinks.	These will decrease his appetite for food.
5 Offer two courses at meals: one savoury course followed by a sweet course.	This gives two opportunities for him to take in the calories and nutrients needed and offers a wider variety of foods. It also makes the meal more interesting.
6 Offer at least one food you know he will eat at each meal.	You can be sure he will eat something even if he refuses all the other foods.
7 Praise him when he eats well.	Babies respond positively to praise.
8 Make positive comments about the food.	Parents and carers are strong role models. If you make positive comments about foods, babies will be more willing to try them.
9 Offer finger foods as often as possible.	Babies enjoy having the control of feeding themselves with finger foods.
10 Eat in a calm, relaxed environment without distractions such as TV, games and toys.	Babies concentrate on one thing at a time. Distractions make it more difficult to concentrate on eating.
11 Finish the meal within about 20–30 minutes and accept that after this he is not going to eat any more.	Carrying the meal on for too long is unlikely to result in him eating much more. It is better to wait for the next snack or meal and offer nutritious foods then.
12 Take away uneaten food without comment.	Accept that he has eaten enough.

Do	Reason
13 Make a list of all the food he does eat over a week and then review it.	If there are foods from all the food groups and some variety within each group then you can reassure yourself that the problem may not be as bad as you thought.
14 Learn to recognize the signs that he has had enough to eat.	He is saying he has had enough food when he: ▶ says no ▶ keeps his mouth shut when food is offered ▶ turns his head away from food being offered ▶ pushes away a spoon, bowl or plate containing food ▶ holds food in his mouth and refuses to swallow it ▶ spits food out repeatedly ▶ cries, shouts or screams ▶ gags or retches.

Don't	Reason
1 Insist that he finishes everything on his plate.	Toddlers should be allowed to eat to their appetite and parents and carers should respect this.
2 Pressure him to eat more when he has indicated to you that he has had enough.	Allow them to eat to their own appetite; they need to learn to know when they are full.

(Contd)

Don't	Reason
3 Take away a refused meal and offer a completely different one in its place.	He will soon take advantage if you do this. In the long run it is better to offer family meals and accept that he will prefer some foods to others. Always try to offer one food at each meal that you know he will eat.
4 Offer the sweet course as a reward.	You will make the sweet course seem more desirable.
5 Offer large drinks of milk, squash or fruit juice within an hour of the meal.	Large drinks will reduce your baby's appetite for the meal. Give water instead.
6 Offer snacks just before a meal.	The snacks will stop him feeling hungry.
7 Give a snack very soon after a meal if he hasn't eaten well at the meal.	Many parents may do this just to ensure their baby has eaten something. However, it is best to have a set meal pattern and wait until the next planned snack or meal before offering food again.
8 Assume that because he has refused a food he will never eat it again.	Tastes change with time. Some babies need to be offered a new food more than ten times before they feel confident to try it.
9 Feel guilty if one meal turns into a disaster.	Put it behind you and approach the next meal positively. Parents also learn by making mistakes.

Cutting back on too much milk, fruit juice and other sweet drinks

About six to eight small drinks per day is enough – offer a drink with each meal and snack. An average drink for a baby over 12 months is about 100–120 ml/3½–4 fl oz in a cup or beaker. Drinks in feeding bottles should have been phased out by 12 months or soon afterwards.

TOO MUCH MILK

If he is having too much milk from cups, put less in the cup. Limit it to 100–120 ml/3½–4 fl oz. If he stubbornly insists on large milk drinks in a bottle, then reducing the amount of milk can be more difficult, especially if he associates the bottle of milk with comfort.

Try breaking the pattern by taking him out of the house at times when he usually has a bottle of milk and give him some food and a small cup of milk instead, i.e. less milk than he usually has in his bottle. You can then begin offering a cup rather than a bottle at home.

The evening bottle at bedtime can be more difficult for him to relinquish, but it is less likely to affect the amount of food he eats during the day. As he becomes used to cups of milk during the day he may become more amenable to changing to a cup of milk in the evening.

Night-time feeding should be avoided because this will reduce a baby's appetite for food during the day. If he habitually wakes for a bottle during the night, the volume of milk should be gradually reduced until he has started to eat more during the day. You can do this by reducing the volume or gradually diluting the milk with water.

Aim to eventually limit milk and milk products to three servings per day.

TOO MANY SWEET DRINKS

Sweet drinks such as fruit juices, squashes and fizzy drinks suppress appetite for food because of the sugar they contain. If your baby refuses to drink water and stubbornly insists on a sweetened drink such as fruit juice or squash then dilute the drinks with more and more water over time so that they become used to very dilute drinks which will contain less sugar.

Fizzy drinks are very damaging for teeth and should not be given to babies. Say no and stick to your decision in the knowledge you are preventing a miserable time at the dentist in the future.

END-OF-CHAPTER QUESTIONS

1 Why do most young toddlers go through a fussy, faddy eating stage?

2 What is food neophobia?

3 Is food neophobia a normal stage of development?

4 When is food neophobia most noticeable?

5 Do all babies grow out of food neophobia with time?

6 What are the medical reasons that may cause your baby to eat poorly?

7 What are the non-medical reasons that may cause your baby to eat poorly

8 Why might your baby refuse to eat particular foods?

9 How do some parents commonly exacerbate food battles?

10 Why do some parents become over anxious about how much food their baby eats?

9

....

Other food-related problems in babies

In this chapter you will learn:
- *normal expectations of weight gain*
- *about food allergies and intolerances*
- *about coeliac disease*
- *about iron deficiency anaemia*
- *about vitamin D deficiency and rickets*
- *about dental decay and erosion*
- *about the causes of constipation*
- *about reflux*
- *how developmental decay can affect eating.*

Many parents worry that children will not be having enough food or growing adequately. Child health records all have height and weight charts and if you have concerns then the first thing to do is have your baby or toddler weighed and measured so that these measures can be plotted on the growth charts.

Is he growing normally?

Your baby will be weighed at birth, during the first week at about five days, at the end of the second week and thereafter when he has his immunizations. It is not necessary to weigh him more frequently than this unless you or your health visitor have any concerns about him. When he is weighed, ask your health visitor to use scales that are calibrated regularly to make sure the measurements are accurate. Babies should be weighed nude without even a nappy. If their length is measured this should also be done nude without a nappy. It is difficult to measure length accurately and two people will need to do it. You may be asked to hold his head against a head board while the health visitor flattens his knees and flexes his feet so they are at 90 degrees to his legs and then brings a measuring board up to the flat soles of his flexed feet.

Having your baby weighed frequently can sometimes cause unnecessary worry if the changes in weight are very small. Babies should not be weighed or measured more frequently than:

▶ *every month for a baby under six months*
▶ *every two months for babies from six to 12 months*
▶ *every three months for a baby over 12 months.*

If he is weighed very frequently the weight difference will be so small that it can be masked by whether your baby has just had a drink or a meal or has just passed urine or a stool.

Weight and length increase most rapidly between birth and six months and after that they begin to slow down. Average length and weight gains are shown in the table opposite.

Average growth rates in babies and toddlers		
Age	Weight gain	Length increase
0–12 months	6.6 kg/14½ lb	25 cm/10 in
1–2 yrs	2.4 kg/5 lb	12 cm/5 in
2–3 yrs	2.0 kg/4½ lb	8 cm/3 in

How babies grow in length is largely determined by their genes which they have inherited from their parents. Babies with tall parents will be longer and weigh more than other babies of the same age. Likewise babies with short parents will tend to be shorter and weigh less than other babies of the same age.

If your baby is growing normally then his weight will rise along the chart roughly parallel to the centile lines marked on the growth chart. However, in the first two months the weight of heavy babies may change towards the middle of the chart and the weight of light babies may move towards the centre line. This is quite normal and these changes are often seen over this time.

The head circumference of your baby should have been measured after he was born and then again at the six-week check. After this it is not necessary unless there are concerns about his development.

If your baby is not growing as expected there are a number of diseases and conditions that could be causing this. These include:

- *diseases which prevent him from absorbing all the nutrients in his milk and food, e.g. coeliac disease and cystic fibrosis*
- *food allergy or intolerance*
- *iron deficiency anaemia*
- *vitamin D deficiency*
- *constipation*
- *gastro-oesophageal reflux.*

Food allergies and intolerances

Although most people use the term 'food allergy' loosely to cover all unpleasant reactions to food, experts have now classified different reactions to food based on how the body is responding to the food. Food hypersensitivity is now the term used to cover all the different types of reaction and food allergy is part of that.

FOOD ALLERGY

The protein in a food triggers a baby's own immune system to respond in a variety of ways. It may be a rapid, severe response or a slower, less severe response depending on whether the antibody IgE is released by the immune system or not. Not everyone makes

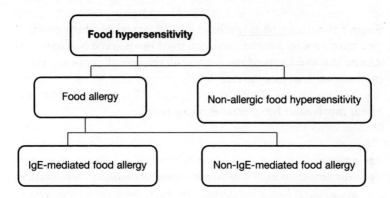

IgE and those people who do are called atopic. Babies at most risk of allergy are those from an atopic family. That is a baby who has a parent or sibling with a food allergy, asthma, eczema or hay fever.

IgE-mediated food allergy
In babies who do make the antibody IgE, a protein in the food reacts with the IgE and one or more of the following symptoms will appear very quickly:

- *rashes*
- *hives*
- *itching*
- *redness*
- *swelling of lips, tongue, face*
- *breathing difficulties*
- *pallor*
- *asthma*
- *projectile vomiting*
- *diarrhoea*
- *wheezing.*

The most serious reaction, known as anaphylaxis, can lead to breathing problems, heart failure and a rapid drop in blood pressure. Babies who suffer in this way need immediate medical attention. Not all babies allergic to food will react this way.

Parents of babies who might have this anaphylactic reaction will be taught how to use an EpiPen (an injection-pen containing adrenaline) and given one to carry with them at all times so that they can use it in an emergency.

Foods involved in IgE-mediated allergies
In most cases these include:

- *peanuts*
- *tree nuts such as almonds, hazelnuts, walnuts, cashew nuts, pecan nuts, Brazil nuts, pistachio nuts, macadamia nuts and Queensland nuts*
- *fish*
- *shellfish*
- *sesame*
- *egg.*

In some cases these include:

- *milk.*

And rarely, these include:

- *wheat*
- *soya.*

Non-IgE-mediated food allergy
When antibodies other than IgE are involved, the reaction to the food appears more slowly – usually a few hours after eating the food. The typical symptoms are:

- *eczema*
- *diarrhoea*
- *constipation*
- *vomiting (a few hours after a meal)*
- *reflux*
- *wheezing*
- *abdominal pain or colic, bloating and wind.*

Foods that cause non-IgE-mediated allergy
In a large number of cases these include:

▶ *milk*
▶ *soya*
▶ *wheat.*

And rarely, these include:

▶ *peanuts*
▶ *tree nuts*
▶ *fish*
▶ *shellfish*
▶ *sesame*
▶ *egg.*

Insight

Food allergies with these slow onset symptoms are the most difficult to diagnose properly.

NON-ALLERGIC FOOD HYPERSENSITIVITY OR FOOD INTOLERANCE

In food intolerance a baby's immune system does not respond to the food but an unpleasant reaction to food still occurs. The symptoms can appear quickly but are rarely life-threatening. Foods which can cause these include:

▶ *Milk – babies who are intolerant lack the enzyme lactase and they are unable to digest lactose which is the sugar in all milks and infant formulas. Lactose intolerance causes diarrhoea, wind and stomach cramps.*
▶ *Citrus fruits – these sometimes contain high levels of benzoic acid which can cause a harmless flare reaction around the mouth.*
▶ *Foods containing salicylates (certain fruits and vegetables) or histamines (e.g. cheese, fish, tomatoes) can cause reactions similar to food allergies such as hives and skin rashes, even facial swelling in some babies.*

- *Foods containing biogenic amines can cause a headache, nausea and giddiness. They include:*
  - ▷ *cheese, especially if matured*
  - ▷ *fermented foods, such as blue cheese, sauerkraut, fermented soya products*
  - ▷ *yeast extracts*
  - ▷ *fish, especially if stale or pickled*
  - ▷ *microbially contaminated foods*
  - ▷ *chocolate*
  - ▷ *some fruits especially citrus fruits, bananas and avocado pears.*

Whether additives in food such as artificial colours and preservatives cause reactions is currently unclear and needs further investigation. You should avoid giving babies any foods or drinks containing:

Colours:

Tartrazine E102
Ponceau 4 R E124
Sunset yellow E110
Carmosine E122
Quinoline yellow E104
Allura red AC E129

Preservatives:

Sodium benzoate E211

How common are food allergies?

Many parents worry that their baby is sensitive to their milk or a particular food but few babies are – only about one baby in 12 has a reaction to food.

Food allergies and intolerances are very distressing for babies and parents but not all of them will last throughout your baby's life. Most babies grow out of it by the time they are around three years old. Only about two in 100 babies remain allergic to one or more foods as they get older.

Insight

I often meet parents of babies over 12 months who are still following a restricted diet long after the baby has grown out of the allergy. This is a shame as food restrictions make life difficult when out and at nursery.

Finding out if your baby has a food allergy or intolerance

Babies may have some of the symptoms already listed but they will not always be caused by a reaction to food. For example, less than half of babies with eczema have this skin condition because of a reaction to food. It can be difficult to determine when the symptoms are due to food and when they are not. It is important that you do not just cut foods out of your baby's diet as you may be inadvertently cutting out key nutrients that he needs for growing and developing. If you suspect he is reacting to milk or another food talk first to your GP or health visitor who can refer you to a paediatrician or an allergy clinic.

Blood tests and skin prick tests will help in diagnosing an IgE-mediated food allergy. These will suggest likely foods that may be causing the problem. However, the only true way to diagnose a food allergy is to remove the suspect food from your baby's diet for about two weeks to see if the symptoms improve. If they do, then the suspect food can be given to your baby again to see if the symptoms come back. A doctor will decide when that food should be reintroduced to your baby. If the reaction is likely to be rapid and severe then this step may need to happen in a hospital where immediate treatment can be given if your baby needs it.

SEEK RELIABLE ADVICE TO MAKE SURE YOUR BABY CONTINUES TO GROW AND DEVELOP NORMALLY

It is very important that the diagnosis of food allergies and intolerances is made by a medical professional such as a medical doctor or registered dietician. They are able to prescribe special milks if your baby needs one. A dietician will be able to discuss weaning foods and family foods that you can include to make sure your baby gets all the nutrients he needs.

Do not take advice from a nutritionist unless he/she is registered with the Health Professions Council or the Nutrition Society. Anyone can call themselves a nutritionist and although some are well qualified and registered with the Nutrition Society, many have dubious qualifications and could give you advice that could harm your baby.

A doctor can prescribe an EpiPen for babies with severe food allergies. This is an injection-pen containing adrenaline, which treats or avoids the severe breathing difficulties and collapse that can arise if there is an anaphylactic reaction to food.

Insight

If your baby is at nursery then you will need to have an extra EpiPen to leave at nursery in case your baby has an anaphylactic reaction there.

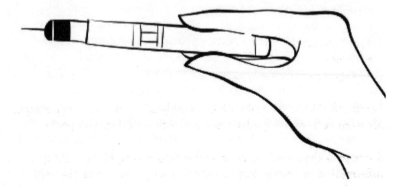

Figure 9.1 An EpiPen.

Coeliac disease

Coeliac disease is an auto-immune disease, not a food allergy or intolerance. However, babies who are diagnosed with coeliac disease must avoid all foods containing gluten – that is any food containing wheat, rye or barley. Some babies with coeliac disease also need to avoid nuts.

Buying food for babies with food allergies or intolerances

European legislation now requires that all pre-packed food must be clearly labelled if it contains any of the following ingredients that can cause a reaction in some people:

▶ *cereals containing gluten (i.e. wheat, rye, barley, oats, spelt, kamut or their hybridized strains)*
▶ *eggs*
▶ *fish and shellfish*
▶ *peanuts*
▶ *soy beans*
▶ *milk and lactose*
▶ *nuts*
▶ *celery*
▶ *mustard*
▶ *sesame seeds*
▶ *lupins*
▶ *sulphur dioxide and sulphites.*

Foods sold loose, in small packages and bottles, and catering packages are exempt from this guidance so do not buy food in multipacks.

Some packaged foods, especially weaning foods, provide allergen information on the package such as: 'This product contains milk, egg, wheat, etc.'

This information is not legally required and may not always be relied on – you always need to check by reading the ingredients list. The ingredients that need to be avoided if your baby has to avoid a food are shown in the following table.

Food to avoid	Ingredients to avoid
Milk	Butter, casein, cheese, cow/sheep/goats' milk, evaporated or condensed milk, cream, curd, ghee, lactoglobulin, lactose, milk solids, whey, yogurt milk proteins.
Egg	Albumin, dried egg, egg powder, egg protein, egg white and yolk, frozen egg, globulin, lecithin (E322), livetin, ovalbumin, ovoglobulin, ovomucin, ovovitellin, pasteurized egg, vitellin.
Wheat	Bran, cereal filler, farina, flour, starch, vegetable protein, wheat, durum wheat, semolina, couscous.
Fish	Anchovy, Worcestershire sauce, aspic, caviar.
Peanuts	Peanuts, peanut oil which could also be called arachis oil or hypogeaia, peanut flour, peanut protein. It is best to avoid all other nuts as well as they may be contaminated with small amounts of peanuts.
Other nuts	Almonds, hazelnuts, walnuts, cashews, pecan nuts, Brazil nuts, pistachio nuts, macadamia nuts and Queensland nuts.
Soya	Hydrolysed vegetable protein, soya lecithin, soya sauce, miso, soya albumin, soya beans, soya flour, soya milk, soya nuts, soya oil, soya proteins, soya sprouts, tempeh, texturized vegetable protein, tofu.

Insight
A baby with a food allergy makes life more complicated, but once the shopping is organized it becomes much easier.

Iron deficiency anaemia

Iron is an essential part of the pigment in red blood cells called haemoglobin, which carries oxygen around the body. From birth until two years old babies are growing very rapidly and developing mentally as well – their brain is also still growing rapidly. Babies under one year old are unlikely to get iron deficiency anaemia if they are breastfed or given infant formula until 12 months of age. Breast milk has a low amount of iron but it is in a form very easily absorbed. Infant formula is enriched with iron to make sure babies get enough. Cows' milk is very low in iron and it is to prevent iron deficiency anaemia that mothers are advised not to change to cows' milk as the main milk drink before their baby's first birthday. By their first birthday babies should be eating a variety of iron rich foods to supply enough iron.

After their first birthday about one in eight babies does not eat enough iron rich foods and goes on to get iron deficiency anaemia. This usually occurs between 18 months and two years. There are some rare causes of iron deficiency anaemia but most babies become anaemic because there is not enough iron in their diet. It is a time when babies become fussy about what food they will eat and unless they are familiar with iron rich foods by their first birthday they may be wary of eating them when they are introduced during their second year.

Causes of iron deficiency anaemia in babies

Babies aged one or two who are most likely to get iron deficiency anaemia are those who:

▶ *eat very few iron rich foods*
▶ *still drink too much milk and consequently eat less foods containing iron*
▶ *were changed onto cows' milk as a main drink before 12 months of age*
▶ *are very fussy about foods particularly those containing good amounts of iron*

(Contd)

Babies with anaemia may become pale and tired and have less resistance to infection, although sometimes there are no apparent symptoms. They may also lose their appetite. Undetected iron deficiency anaemia can cause slow growth and developmental delay. A blood test is needed to determine if a baby is iron deficient but this can now be done with just a finger prick to extract a couple of drops of blood. If iron deficiency is confirmed your doctor can prescribe an iron supplement to treat the deficiency which will resolve over the next few weeks. Whether the effects of slow growth and delayed development affect the baby as he gets older is still debatable. Some studies have shown that children who had iron deficiency anaemia as a baby have lower IQs later in childhood. However, other studies show there is no difference.

PREVENTING IRON DEFICIENCY ANAEMIA

The two most important steps you can make to prevent your baby getting anaemia are to:

1 *Make sure your baby learns to like foods rich in iron between six and 12 months, i.e. before they become fussy eaters in their second year.*
2 *Cut back your baby's intake of milk to about three cups of milk per day after his first birthday so that he is less reliant on milk and will eat more food. Servings of yogurt and cheese can be substituted for each of these three cups of milk.*

The foods that provide the best source of iron are red meat such as beef, lamb and pork. Dark poultry meat such as chicken legs and thighs and oily fish are also good sources. This is because they provide iron in a readily absorbable form, that is, as haem iron. Liver is a very rich source of haem iron but should only be offered once a week as all liver now contains very high levels of vitamin A.

Other foods with iron provide it in the form known as non-haem iron which is less readily absorbed but this can be improved by having foods high in vitamin C at the same time. Foods rich in non-haem iron are pulses, nuts, fortified breakfast cereals and some vegetables. Follow-on formulas and growing-up milks also contain this form of iron.

Good sources of iron	Haem iron content per serving (mg)
15 g/½ oz liver	1.4
25 g/1 oz lean beef	0.7
25 g/1 oz lean lamb	0.5
25 g/1 oz lean pork	0.2
25 g/1 oz dark poultry meat	0.2
25 g/1 oz chicken breast	0.1

	Non-haem iron content per serving (mg)
15 g/½ oz fortified breakfast cereal	1.8
1 small egg	1.0
15 g/½ oz (approx. 4) dried apricots	0.5
20 g/¾ oz steamed/fried tofu	0.5
1 small slice white bread	0.4
15 g/½ oz cooked lentils	0.4
20 g/¾ oz (cooked) chickpeas – mashed	0.3
1 small banana	0.3
15 g/½ oz cooked broccoli	0.15
30 g/1 oz mashed potato	0.1

Insight

About one in eight babies over 12 months in the UK gets iron deficiency anaemia through eating a poor diet.

Vitamin D deficiency and rickets

Vitamin D is a fat-soluble vitamin that is essential for bone growth and general health. It helps calcium absorption from milk and foods and controls the deposition of calcium and other minerals into bone. Vitamin D is also important in boosting the immune system and protecting toddlers against infections.

Vitamin D is sometimes called the sunshine vitamin as most vitamin D is made in our skins when we are outside in daylight. Very few foods contain vitamin D – oily fish is the best source. Margarines, follow-on formulas and one or two breakfast cereals are fortified with vitamin D. Meat and egg yolks only contain tiny amounts.

In the UK sunlight is only strong enough to make vitamin D in the skin between April and September and we need to make enough in these months to last us through the winter. Nowadays, many of us spend little time outside, especially those with office jobs and work that keeps us indoors. Studies show that about one in four women of child bearing age has low vitamin D levels.

Blood tests to check vitamin D levels are not done routinely on pregnant women so there is no way of knowing what your vitamin D stores were at the beginning of your pregnancy or during it. Mothers most likely to have low vitamin D stores are:

▶ *those with dark pigmented skins because they are less efficient at making vitamin D in their skin than mothers with white skin*
▶ *those who spend little time outside, e.g. office and shop workers*
▶ *those who cover their skin when they are outside*
▶ *those living in northern areas of the UK because the further you live from the equator the less vitamin D you make in your skin when outside.*

If you had low stores yourself during your pregnancy, your baby will have been born with a low store of vitamin D.

Babies who are born with very low vitamin D levels may have fits due to low calcium in their blood in the first few weeks of life. Older babies may have poor bone development and go on to develop rickets in which the bones become soft and misshapen.

Dark-skinned babies of Asian, African, Afro-Caribbean and Middle-Eastern origin are more likely to have vitamin D deficiency than caucasian babies.

To prevent vitamin D deficiency the Department of Health recommends:

▶ *a daily supplement of vitamin D for all pregnant and breastfeeding mothers*
▶ *a daily supplement of vitamins A and D for breastfed babies from six months, but babies at risk of vitamin D deficiency because their mother may have had low vitamin D stores during pregnancy should begin at birth or at one month of life. Formula milk has vitamin D added to it and babies drinking formula milk should begin a supplement from the time they are drinking less than 500 ml/17 fl oz of formula milk each day.*

The daily dose of the NHS Healthy Start Children's vitamin drops provides 233 μg vitamin A and 7.5 μg vitamin D. If you can't get this supplement, look for one with similar amounts in it.

Dental problems

Caring for your baby's first set of teeth is essential to prevent any dental decay and erosion of the tooth enamel. Either of these can cause pain to your baby. These first teeth help with the development of speech and allow optimum growth of the jaw so that the second permanent set of teeth which come later in childhood can grow and develop normally in the gums.

Oral hygiene should begin before the age of one year. You need to begin cleaning your baby's teeth with a soft toothbrush and a smear of toothpaste containing fluoride at least twice each day from the time they first appear.

DENTAL DECAY

The foods most likely to cause decay are sugary foods. Sugary foods are not recommended under the age of 12 months but after this they can be included in meals but should not be given as snacks.

Tooth decay is most likely in babies who:

- *eat or drink sweet foods and/or drinks including fruit juice more than four times per day*
- *graze on food throughout the day*
- *continue to drink from bottles after 12 months of age*
- *are given a bottle of a sweet drink or milk when put into bed.*

Saliva in the mouth protects against tooth decay. During sleep salivary flow and swallowing decline, making food and sugars more damaging because they remain in the mouth for longer.

DENTAL EROSION

The tooth enamel of babies is very delicate and can easily be eroded if acidic food and drinks are eaten frequently. Acidic drinks are fruit juices, squashes and fizzy drinks. Water and milk are not acidic and are the only safe drinks to offer between meals. It is best not to offer squashes and fizzy drinks and to encourage your baby to drink water instead. Fruit juices can be an enjoyable drink for toddlers and are useful for providing vitamin C to help iron absorption, especially with vegetarian meals. As long as they are well diluted and only offered in cups at mealtimes they will not be harmful.

Insight

I often see parents who think they are taking great care of their baby's or toddler's teeth and are astonished to find that drinking fruit juices has caused decay. Some babies sip on these frequently during the day.

Constipation

Young babies may pass a stool several times a day but once babies are over 12 months the frequency of passing a stool may vary from once or twice each day to once every two days. Anything within this range is considered normal. Constipated babies pass stools less frequently than this and the stool is very hard and dry. Babies may strain excessively to pass a stool and they may cry with the pain when passing it.

BABIES UNDER SIX MONTHS

Breastfed babies are unlikely to get constipation but some babies on formula milk become constipated. If your baby is one of these check that you are making up the formula milk exactly to the instructions on the tin. If you are making up the milk by adding too many scoops of powder, overfilling the scoops of powder or packing down the powder too tightly into the scoop then you may be making up feeds that are too concentrated. This can cause constipation.

Once you begin weaning your baby onto solid food you may find that the constipation resolves on its own as your baby begins to eat foods with more fibre, i.e. fruit, vegetables and cereals. Make sure you offer your baby a cup of water with each of his meals once he is eating more than just a few teaspoons of food.

BABIES OVER 12 MONTHS

Too little fluid or too little fibre may be the reason for constipation. If your baby is over 12 months and has constipation check he is having:

▶ *About six to eight drinks per day of about 100–120 ml/3–4 oz. This will be a drink with each meal and one in between the meals*

▶ *Fruit and vegetables at every meal: make sure you are giving your baby fruit at breakfast and at least one vegetable and one fruit at the other two meals.*

▶ *Potatoes or cereal-based food at each meal. Cereal-based foods are pasta, rice, couscous and anything made with flour. You could change to offering more wholegrain cereals such as Weetabix, Shredded Wheat or Cherrios for breakfast. You could also include some more wholemeal bread and crackers. However, do not offer bran or cereals enriched with bran as bran can decrease the absorption of some of the valuable nutrients in food that your baby needs.*

If the constipation continues to be a problem you should talk to your GP who can prescribe a simple laxative or stool softener to ease the passage of hard stool. In rare cases an anal fissure may be causing constipation. This is a tear of the anal passage which can be treated.

If constipation in babies over 12 months is not resolved quickly, babies may begin to withhold stools to avoid the pain of passing them. This can then set up chronic constipation and your baby will become less aware of when his rectum is full and when he needs to pass a stool. Chronic constipation as babies become older can be more difficult to resolve.

Insight

I do see babies who are eating and drinking well but get constipation anyway. Sometimes doctors suggest a trial of a milk-free diet but this resolves the constipation in only a few babies.

Reflux

As discussed in Chapter 1, many babies have some reflux in the first few weeks of life and posseting after a feed is normal. Very few babies continue to suffer reflux as they get older but for those who do, feeding can still be associated with pain. Smaller meals more frequently may make it easier for them to eat enough.

6–12 MONTHS

You may find that giving meals and milk-feeds separately will be more comfortable for your baby.

Routine example

On waking 6:30 a.m.–7 a.m.: Breast or bottle-feed.

8 a.m. breakfast: Baby cereal or porridge and mashed fruit and milk or egg with bread or toast.

 Finger foods: soft fruit slices or toast crusts.

9:30 a.m.: Breast or bottle-feed.

10 a.m. sleep for about an hour

12:00–1 p.m. lunch: First course: mashed meat or pulses with mashed potato or rice and with mashed vegetables.

 Finger foods: soft vegetable sticks.

 Second course: mashed fruit with milk-based pudding.

 Finger foods: soft fruit slices.

2:30 p.m.: Breastfeed or milk-feed in a bottle or cup.

3:00 p.m. sleep for about an hour

4:30 p.m. tea: First course: mashed fish with mashed vegetables, or scrambled eggs with bread or toast, or pasta with cheese or vegetable sauce or chapatti with mild curry.

 Finger foods: soft vegetable sticks or cooked pasta pieces.

 Second course: mashed fruit.

 Finger foods: soft fruit slices.

(Contd)

5:30 p.m:	Breastfeed or milk-feed in a bottle or cup.
6:30 p.m. bath and bedtime routine	
7:30 p.m:	Breastfeed or bottle of formula.
7:45 p.m. into bed	

OVER 12 MONTHS

Rather than bigger meals and small snacks, give three small meals and two to three nutritious snacks.

Routine example

Early morning:	Wakes – no milk-feed.
7 a.m. breakfast:	Cereal and milk and fruit or egg and toast with fruit juice.
9:30 a.m. snack:	Sandwich and cup of milk.
10:30 a.m. sleep	
12:00 lunch:	One savoury course with finger foods. Water to drink with the meal.
2 p.m. snack:	Yogurt or milk pudding with fruit fingers and drink of water.
2:30 p.m. sleep	
3:30 p.m. snack:	Crumpet with honey and small cup of milk.
6:30 p.m. tea:	Small savoury course with finger foods. Fruit fingers. Water in a cup with the meal.
Bedtime routine:	Cup of milk.

Insight

I have a lot of sympathy for parents of babies who suffer with reflux. It is distressing to see babies in so much pain, and laundry turns into a mountain every day as feeds and meals are regurgitated over both parent and baby. However, once babies grow out of it there do not seem to be any long-lasting effects.

Developmental delay

Occasionally some babies find it difficult to move on from puréed or well mashed food to lumpy foods and then minced and chopped foods. They may continue to frequently gag or choke on food beyond the age of nine or ten months when they should be managing lumps in food well. These babies may have some developmental delay and may need some help from a speech and language therapist. If you are concerned that your baby is not progressing as expected then talk to your health visitor or GP.

END-OF-CHAPTER QUESTIONS

1   *Do babies gain more or less weight in their second year compared with their first year?*

2   *How common is food allergy in babies?*

3   *Around what age do most babies grow out of their food allergy?*

4   *Do all babies with a food allergy need an EpiPen?*

5   *Which drinks are acidic and if drunk frequently will cause dental erosion?*

6   *Which babies are most likely to get iron deficiency anaemia?*

7   *What type of meal routine do babies with reflux prefer?*

8   *Are breastfed or formula-fed babies more likely to have constipation?*

9   *Which babies are most at risk of rickets?*

10 *Which vitamin supplement is recommended for all babies?*

10

Buying food for your baby

In this chapter you will learn:
- *about different kinds of food*
- *which fats are the best*
- *about vitamins and fortified foods.*

Formula milks

The composition of these milks is very tightly controlled by European legislation to prevent anything that might harm your baby being added. There is little difference between the small range of standard milks that are sold in the UK, but as research into formula milks progresses different brands make different claims depending on the minor modifications they make. However, changing from one brand of milk to another does not usually benefit your baby.

Insight
When parents are anxious about their baby's discomfort their only option seems to be to change the milk. Sometimes parents report an improvement after changing, but it is more likely that changing the milk has coincided with the baby getting better on his own.

Commercial baby foods

The composition of baby cereals and tins and jars of pre-prepared food for babies are also fairly tightly controlled by European legislation to make sure they provide a minimum level of key nutrients and a regulated maximum level of salt, added sugar, additives and pesticides. Unfortunately, the manufacturers only add the minimum levels of meat allowed which means they are not a rich source of iron. Those labelled as meat and vegetable have to have a minimum of ten per cent meat while those labelled vegetable and meat only have to contain eight per cent meat. Choose the former or add some extra meat to make them more nutritious for your baby.

Halal commercial baby foods are now available for Muslim parents who wish to wean their babies on halal meat. Only one company makes them in the UK: Mumtaz.

The amount of sugar that can be added to baby foods is strictly limited.

Buying family foods for babies

Supermarkets now offer us a huge range of foods all year round. Although this means we have a considerable choice there are compromises in this. Many of us no longer know when foods are in season which is when they have the best flavour and more nutrients because storage time is minimal. In some areas farmers' markets selling locally grown produce are now reinstating this choice. Seasonal food is generally cheaper and higher in two vitamins – folic acid and vitamin C because they both deteriorate with long storage times. Minerals and phytochemicals are not affected.

When buying fresh foods choose the freshest possible to minimize the time the food has been stored. Choose organic or foods that have been grown with the least amount of additives, pesticides and hormone treatments for yourself if you are breastfeeding and for your baby.

Genetically modified (GM) foods

Genetic modification of foods involves changing the genetic material of the plant or animal to alter one specific trait of that food. The modification is usually done to improve the yield of the crop or to make it resistant to a pest or infection to which the crop is normally susceptible. The nutritional content of the food is not usually changed and strict controls are in place, such that each modified product is thoroughly assessed for any difference from its conventional counterpart.

Since 1996, GM soya, maize, oilseed rape and other crops, have been eaten on a regular basis by hundreds of millions of people and animals in the United States and there has been no substantiated case of harm arising from their consumption. However, there remain concerns that we do not know enough about the science or any possible long-term effects of consuming GM foods. Unforeseen problems could still occur. In the UK most supermarkets have opted not to stock GM products.

Organic versus non-organic

Organic food is produced without the use of most agrochemicals. Naturally occurring fertilizers and pesticides are allowed but all other pesticides, herbicides and genetically modified organisms which have mostly been developed in the last 40 years are banned. Organic food has a much shorter shelf life and storage times are minimized. Because of this, organic foods may have slightly more folic acid and vitamin C as these two nutrients deteriorate with long storage times. Organic and non-organic food contain similar amounts of all other nutrients. Although each pesticide used in the food industry is checked for safety, the effects of ingesting combinations of different pesticide residues that a family might consume in a meal of several different foods has not been checked. This is of more concern in babies who are growing and developing and would be more susceptible to any effects.

Organic regulations do not allow for genetically modified ingredients to be included.

Salt and sodium

Salt contains sodium, too much of which can cause high blood pressure in later life if children carry on always eating very salty food. Babies need a certain amount of sodium in order to grow and breast milk and formula milks contain the correct amount of sodium for the first six months of life. Commercial baby foods do not contain added salt because regulations do not allow it to be added to baby food. If you are buying foods that are not specifically labelled for babies then choose those lower in sodium when you have a choice. Some foods naturally contain sodium, e.g. milk and milk products, meat, bread and cheese. These foods are important for your baby because of the other nutrients they contain so don't cut out all foods that show sodium on the label. Do not give your baby under 12 months obviously salty foods such as bacon, crisps and salted snacks, and tinned food with added salt. For babies over 12 months the Food Standards Agency recommends a maximum of 2.0 g salt or 0.4 g sodium per day. This is impossible for parents to calculate but means that salty foods such as

▶ *crisps and salty snacks*
▶ *processed meats, e.g. nuggets, burgers*
▶ *tinned spaghetti and baked beans in sauce*
▶ *potato waffles, smiles, etc.*

should only be given very occasionally. Use herbs and spices in your own cooking rather than salt and do not add salt to food at the table.

Insight

I find the low salt messages have made parents quite scared of giving salty foods to babies and young children. In fact, from about six months, babies' kidneys can cope with salty foods very well and no harm will come to babies who eat them in small amounts. It is best not to encourage a preference for salty foods in babies so that they continue to choose them over other foods as they get older.

Which fats are the best?

Babies need a lot of fat in their first few months. It is a good source of energy for them and fats are an integral part of the membrane around each cell. Of the dry weight of the brain, 70 per cent is fat. Both breast milk and formula milks contain a mixture of all types of fats – saturated, monounsaturated and polyunsaturated. Oils and fats containing higher levels of omega 3 fats are more beneficial for babies.

SATURATED FATS

Babies' early food intake has a lot of saturated fat as it is present in both breast milk and formula milks and for babies saturated fat is not harmful. It is an integral part of important nutrient-rich foods such as meat, eggs, milk and cheese.

TRANS FATS

In processed foods saturated fat and trans fats are formed when vegetable fats are heated to high temperatures and/or processed, e.g. hydrogenated vegetable oil has all the unsaturated fats changed to saturated, and trans fats are formed in the process. Industrially produced trans and saturated fats should be kept to a minimum by avoiding processed food or keeping it to a minimum and choosing processed foods with very low amounts of saturated and trans fats. Highly-processed foods include:

▶ *high-fat snacks such as crisps*
▶ *processed foods containing hydrogenated vegetable oils: margarines, cakes, biscuits, puddings, ready-made sauces and meals*
▶ *processed foods which have been fried, e.g. crumb-coated fish, chicken and meat products.*

The trans fats naturally present in milk and milk products are not harmful, whereas trans fats produced by industrial processing are now known to raise cholesterol in the same way saturated fat does.

UNSATURATED FATS

Two of the unsaturated fats, omega 3 and omega 6 fats, are essential for babies – they are needed for the developing brain, eyes and nerves in particular. They are most useful in their long-chain form which is EPA, DHA and AA, and all of these are in breast milk and formula milks suitable from birth.

BALANCING OMEGA 3 AND OMEGA 6 FATS IN BABIES' DIETS

Up until about 50 years ago our diets included about equal quantities of these two essential fats but nowadays we eat a much higher proportion of omega 6 fats and very little omega 3 fat. This change is thought to be one of the factors causing increased rates of allergy, asthma and hay fever in children. You can increase your baby's intake of omega 3 fats by including foods naturally rich in omega 3 fats. The best source is oily fish such as salmon, mackerel, trout, fresh tuna, sardines, pilchards and eel. Other good sources are omega 3 rich oils which are flaxseed, rapeseed, walnut, olive and soya oils. Pure vegetable oil is often rapeseed oil and some have the little yellow rapeseed flowers on the label.

Many foods supplemented with omega 3 fats are now appearing on supermarket shelves, e.g. spreads, yogurts, eggs, berry fruit juices, breads, milk, some breakfast cereals and biscuits.

Sugar

Adding sugar to babies' food is not recommended as they naturally prefer sweet foods but need to learn to like other tastes. When buying food it is not easy to determine the amount of sugar that has been added to a food. The total amount of sugar must be displayed on the label. This figure will include natural sugars occurring in food as well as added sugar. The sugars naturally occurring in certain foods are:

▶ *lactose – the sugar in milk*
▶ *fructose – the sugar in fruit*
▶ *maltose – the sugar that is present in small amounts in all starchy foods.*

Additional sugar is usually added to improve flavour and will be added in various forms:

▶ *sucrose*
▶ *dextrose*
▶ *glucose syrup*
▶ *corn syrup*
▶ *fructose*
▶ *golden syrup*
▶ *honey*
▶ *fruit juice concentrate.*

If the added sugar is included in two or three forms they will be placed further down the ingredients list than if all the added sweetness is only included in one form of sugar.

When looking for low-sugar foods, e.g. breakfast cereals, compare the sugar amount per 100 g/4 oz and buy the lower one. However, do not expect any foods to be sugar free because of the natural sugars in most foods. Do remember that food must be enjoyed and a little sugar will do your baby no harm. Small amounts of sugar, particularly in foods that are eaten in small quantities such as tomato ketchup, do not need to be avoided.

Insight

In the same way as I find parents are scared of salt, many are also quite scared of their babies eating any sugar. It is best not to encourage a preference for sweet tastes, but a little sugar in food to make it more palatable does no harm to your baby.

Buying vitamin drops

Vitamin drops for babies containing vitamins A and D are available in all pharmacies and some supermarkets. They can be quite expensive as they usually contain a number of other nutrients which your baby doesn't necessarily need. The NHS Healthy Start Children's vitamin drops contain vitamins A, C and D and are cheaper but are only sold in some NHS child health clinics. Ask your health visitor where to get them.

Additives and sweeteners

The additives and sweeteners used in food have all been tested for safety before being certified by the Food Standards Agency as safe for use by the food industry. Some additives are normally found in foods, e.g. ascorbic acid which is vitamin C and is often used to preserve food. However, there are other additives that have been manufactured and introduced into our environment quite recently and all the various different combinations of them have not been tested and we are all guinea pigs in a way. The long-term effects of using them are not necessarily known. Growing babies are more vulnerable and it is preferable to keep additives to a minimum.

Many drinks contain sweeteners so it is preferable to give your baby diluted, pure fruit juice which does not contain any.

Avoid any drinks or food containing the following as concern that they may affect behaviour has been raised recently:

Colours:

> Tartrazine E102
> Ponceau 4 R E124
> Sunset yellow E110
> Carmosine E122

Quinoline yellow E104
Allura red AC E129

Preservatives:

Sodium benzoate E211

Fortified foods

Fortified foods are those with added nutrients. Sometimes the nutrients added are those that have been lost during the processing of the food, such as:

▶ *iron added to white and brown flour*
▶ *B vitamins and iron added to processed breakfast cereals.*

Functional foods are those with added vitamins and/or minerals that are not necessarily normally contained within that food. Long-standing examples are:

▶ *calcium added to white bread*
▶ *vitamins A and D added to margarine.*

Both these additions were instigated in the 1940s during the Second World War.

Fortified foods are now a growth area in the food industry as, with a higher consumer interest in health and nutrition, added nutrients in foods are increasingly becoming part of the marketing strategy. Recent examples are the addition of:

▶ *omega 3 fats to spreads, yogurts, eggs, berry fruit juices, breads, milk, some breakfast cereals and biscuits*
▶ *vitamin D to fromage frais and cheese*
▶ *calcium to cereal bars*
▶ *pre and probiotics to yogurts and milk desserts.*

Reading a label

Food labels can be confusing and although regulated by law they do not always give the full information. See below for a sample food label explained.

- Information is given as **per 100 g of food** and also as **per portion**. Often these are adult portions so you will need to estimate how much your baby will eat.

- **Protein** is expressed in grams.

- **Fat** is expressed in grams and is the total of saturated, monounsaturated and polyunsaturated. 'Of which saturates' is the amount of saturated fat also given in grams. This fat will be all the fats naturally present in the milk used to make the yogurt as there are no other ingredients that contain fat.

- The ingredients are listed in descending order by the amount used in the recipe. In this example, yogurt is the main ingredient and is 88% of the total ingredients. Natural flavouring is the smallest ingredient added.

Organic raspberry bio live yogurt

Ingredients: Organic Whole Yogurt (88%), Organic Raspberries (5%), Organic Sugar, Organic Lemon Juice, Organic Tapioca Starch, Natural Flavouring

Nutrition Information

Typical values	Per 125 g pot	Per 100 g
Energy	125 Kcal/ 526 KJ	100 Kcal/ 418 KJ
Protein	5.5 g	4.4 g
Carbohydrate	14.4 g	11.5 g
Of which sugars	14.1 g	11.3 g
Fat	5.0 g	4.0 g
Of which saturates	3.1 g	2.5 g
Fibre	0.3 g	0.2 g
Sodium	0.1 g	0.1 g
Calcium	194 mg	155 mg

- **Fibre** is measured in grams. It comes from cereals, fruit and vegetables. This small amount will come from the raspberries.

- **Sodium** is measured in grams. To calculate the equivalent salt content, multiply by 2.5. This small amount is the natural sodium in milk as there is no salt added in making the yogurt.

- **Calcium** is also measured in grams and is that naturally contained in the milk.

- **Carbohydrate** is expressed in grams and will be the total figure for starch and sugar.

- **'Of which sugars'** is expressed in grams and represents the sugar added plus any natural sugars. In this case it includes the natural milk sugar, lactose, as well as the natural fruit sugar, fructose, in the raspberries. The rest will be the added sugar but it is impossible from this information to work out how much sugar is actually added. We know that it will be less than 5% of the total as it is lower down the ingredients list than the raspberries which are shown as being 5% of the weight.

END-OF-CHAPTER QUESTIONS

1   Is there any benefit in changing from one brand of formula milk to another?

2   Name three substances that are limited to a maximum by European regulations on baby foods.

3   Which two vitamins are lower in food that has been stored for a long time?

4   Have genetically modified foods been proved to be harmful?

5   Which essential fat appears in much smaller quantities in our diet than it did about 50 years ago?

6   Which food is the best source of omega 3 fat?

7   Which is the best oil to use for cooking to have a good supply of omega 3 fats?

8   What are the natural sugars found in foods?

9   Which two nutrients are added into white bread?

10 Which two nutrients are added into margarines?

11

Food safety and hygiene

In this chapter you will learn:
- *how to sterilize bottles and make up powdered infant formula*
- *how long to store food in a fridge for babies*
- *how to safely reheat food for babies*
- *which foods to avoid for babies over 12 months.*

Whether you need bottles for expressed breast milk or for formula milk-feeds it is imperative to use sterilized bottles and teats until your baby is 12 months old. It is very difficult to ensure that every trace of milk has been cleaned from a bottle or teat and milk is an ideal medium for bacteria to grow in. Babies can become seriously ill very quickly if there is bacterial infection in their milk.

When you begin to use cups for your baby's milk-feeds, which will be anytime between 6 and 12 months old, as long as you are sure the cup is scrupulously clean and you are putting the milk into the cup just before offering it to your baby, then it is not necessary to sterilize the cup. Cups are much easier to clean thoroughly than a bottle and teat.

Sterilizing bottles and teats for milk-feeds

HOW TO STERILIZE

Clean the bottle, teats, retaining rings and bottle caps in hot soapy water as soon as possible after a feed, using a clean bottle brush.

Squirting water through the teat helps remove every trace of milk. Rinse all the equipment before sterilizing.

COLD WATER STERILIZING

A cold water sterilizing kit comes with a container, floating cover, lid and sachets of sterilizing solution. Follow the manufacturer's instructions to prepare the sterilizing solution.

Change the sterilizing solution every 24 hours.

Leave the bottles, teats, retaining rings and bottle caps in the sterilizing solution for at least 30 minutes.

Make sure there is no air trapped in the bottles or teats when putting them in the sterilizing solution.

Keep all the equipment under the solution with a floating cover.

STEAM STERILIZING

A steam sterilizer is a kit which heats water to produce steam. Follow the manufacturer's instructions.

Make sure the openings of the bottles and teats are facing down in the sterilizer.

Any equipment not used straight away should be re-sterilized before use.

Storing and using expressed breast milk

Express your breast milk directly into a sterilized bottle or container. Cover it with the lid which also should have been sterilized. If you will be using the milk within three to five days you can store it in the fridge. Store it at the back of the fridge which is the coldest part. Do not store milk on the shelves of the fridge door because the temperature may rise above 5°C/41°F if the door is opened frequently. If you need to keep the milk for longer than this then it should be frozen. It can be kept in a freezer compartment of a fridge for up to two weeks or in a separate freezer for up six months.

Making up bottles of formula milk

All formula milks are now available as:

▶ *powders which need to be reconstituted with boiled water that is still hot in a sterilized bottle*
▶ *ready-to-feed liquid formula which can be poured directly into a sterilized bottle.*

The ready-to-feed liquid formula is more expensive but is sterile until the carton is open so is more convenient when you are away from home.

Powdered formula is cheaper to use but is not sterile and manufacturers cannot guarantee that it will not contain traces of bacteria. Although illnesses from feeding babies on formula milks are rare, it is important that powdered formula milks are made up using boiled water which is still above 70°C/158°F – that is, using water that has been boiled and left to cool in the kettle for no longer than 30 minutes. You can use freshly drawn tap water or bottled water but both must be boiled.

Ideally each feed should be made up just before feeding to avoid the likelihood of bacterial contamination increasing during storage. This is more crucial with premature babies, those who are ill and very young babies under about two months of age. These babies will find it more difficult to cope with an illness caused by bacteria which can multiply in stored milk.

Bacterial contamination of a milk-feed can also occur while making the feed because some bacteria which multiply in milk are now ubiquitous in the environment and can be present on all work surfaces in all kitchens – even the cleanest.

STEPS FOR MAKING UP A POWDERED FEED

1 *Before making up a feed, clean the surface you are going to use. It is really important that you wash your hands.*
2 *If you are using a cold water sterilizer, shake off any excess solution from the bottle and the teat or rinse the bottle with boiled water from the kettle.*
3 *Stand the bottle on the clean work surface. Keep the teat and cap on the upturned lid of the sterilizer. Avoid putting them on the work surface.*
4 *When making up infant formula milk use fresh tap water to fill the kettle. Alternatively, you can use bottled water but avoid bottled mineral waters which may contain high levels of minerals.*
5 *Whether using bottled or tap water, boil it in the kettle and then allow it to cool for up to 30 minutes in the kettle. This is to maintain a temperature above 70°C/158°F. Using water over 70°C/158°F will kill most of the bacteria in the powder.*
6 *Put the boiled water in the bottle first and check the water level is correct. Loosely fill the scoop with milk powder and level it off without compacting it.*
7 *Always use one scoop of powder for every 30 ml/1 oz water. Too many scoops may cause your baby to become constipated or dehydrated. Too few scoops will mean your baby is not getting enough nutrients to grow. Always use the scoop that is supplied in the container of milk powder.*
8 *Add the milk powder to the water. Hold the edge of the teat and put it on the bottle. Screw the retaining ring onto the bottle. Cover the teat with a cap and shake the bottle until the powder is dissolved.*
9 *Cool the bottle of milk quickly by holding it under running cold water or standing it in a jug of very cold water. Shake to distribute the heat and test the feed to make sure it is cool enough before giving it to your baby by dripping a few drops onto your wrist.*

Storing formula milk-feeds

If you are going to store made-up bottles of infant formula put them into the back of the fridge where the temperature will be coldest. Do not store them in shelves on the door as foods here do not remain at a constant temperature, particularly if the fridge is opened frequently.

You can store the feeds for up to 24 hours as long as you are confident your fridge is maintained at less than 5°C/41°F. However, long storage times are not ideal and you should aim to store them for as little time as possible by making them up one by one when needed or in very small batches. Discard any feeds that remain after 24 hours.

Insight

The advice to make up formula feeds just before feeding began in 2006. If making up a feed in advance is less stressful for you than making it up in the middle of the night when your baby is awake and screaming for his feed, then do not feel guilty doing that. Just make sure it is cooled quickly and stored in the fridge.

Warming a feed which has been stored in the fridge

Standing the bottle in a jug of hot water is preferable. Heating milk in a microwave oven is dangerous as the milk heats unevenly and continues to heat up after it has been taken out of the microwave.

Shake a reheated feed well to distribute the heat evenly. Before feeding your baby, test the temperature of the milk by dropping a little onto the inside of your wrist. Feed when the milk is at body temperature or slightly cooler (37°C/98.6°F).

Feeding formula milk when you are outside your home

If you are going out for the day and there is nowhere safe to make up feeds the safest option is to take ready-to-feed formula in an unopened carton and take along a sterilized bottle and teat which is capped and sealed immediately after you take it out of the sterilizer. Alternatively you can:

1 *Make up the feed at home, cool it quickly and transport it in a cool bag containing an ice brick. You can use a feed which has been stored this way for up to four hours.*

or:

2 *Measure out the powdered milk into a clean container and fill a thermos flask with boiling water. Take these as well as a sterilized bottle and teat which is capped and sealed immediately after you take it out of the sterilizer. When your baby requires a feed, measure out the boiled water into the sterilized bottle and add the powder. You will then have to cool the bottle of milk before feeding your baby.*

Safe preparation of weaning food

Whether cooking weaning foods or family foods that you will also feed to your baby, the following standard food safety guidelines should be followed:

▶ *Wash hands thoroughly before preparing food.*
▶ *Use clean work surfaces for preparing food.*
▶ *Use a separate chopping board for meat, fish and poultry. Never cut bread, vegetables, fruit or cooked food on a chopping board that has been used for meat, fish or poultry.*

- *Always store cooked and raw food separately in the fridge. Make sure raw meats cannot drip onto cooked food; store cooked food above raw meats.*
- *Cover foods for storage.*
- *Defrost meat, poultry and fish thoroughly in the fridge before cooking.*
- *Reheated food should be heated to piping hot before being cooled for children.*
- *Make sure all meat, poultry, fish and eggs are cooked thoroughly. For meat, this is when the juices run clear when you put a knife into the thickest part of the meat.*
- *Wash fruits and vegetables if being eaten raw.*
- *Do not reheat food more than once.*
- *Keep the temperature of your fridge at 4°C/40°F and your freezer at or below −18°C/0°F.*
- *Do not refreeze food which was frozen and has been partially or completely thawed.*
- *Never use food past its 'use by' date.*
- *Keep dried food in sealed containers and frozen food in airtight containers.*
- *Don't leave foods in the freezer for too long. Use them in rotation and check the freezer manual to see how long each food can safely be frozen.*

Once the food is cooked it can be served immediately or cooled and stored in the fridge for up to 24 hours.

Freezing and reheating food for babies

Weaning food can also be frozen and stored covered in the freezer. Make sure you label the food with the date of preparation so that it is only stored for the length of time recommended for your freezer.

For early weaning foods when you will only be offering small quantities you can put the food into an ice cube tray. Cover the filled ice cube tray with the lid or place the filled ice cube tray into a clean plastic bag and seal it. Stand it in the freezer until frozen. You can then tip these cubes of frozen weaning food into a freezer bag so that you can use the ice tray for another batch of food. Remember to label and date the bags containing the food cubes so that you use it within the time recommended for your freezer.

Thaw the food thoroughly in a covered container in the fridge. Once thawed it can be stored for up to 24 hours in the fridge. When you are preparing your baby's meal, reheat the food to piping hot and then allow to cool. Stir it thoroughly to make sure it is an even temperature and check it is cool enough before feeding it to your baby. Any food not used should be discarded as it shouldn't be refrozen or reheated.

Feeding weaning foods

Bowls, spoons and cups do not need to be sterilized but should be scrupulously clean.

Wash your hands and those of your baby before the meal as you will both be handling food.

Cooked food for young babies can be kept for up to 24 hours in a fridge. Take out a little more than the amount your baby normally eats. Heat the food thoroughly and allow it to cool. Before feeding stir the food to ensure it is all at an even temperature and test that it is at or below body temperature. Any leftover food not wanted by your baby must be discarded at the end of a meal. The bacteria in saliva, which will be mixed into the food from the weaning spoon, can grow in stored food.

Never reheat weaning food which has already been reheated once.

Commercial weaning foods are sterile in the container until opened. If you are not going to use the whole container of food take out the amount you think your baby will eat and the remainder can be stored covered in the fridge for up to 24 hours.

Food safety for one- and two-year-old babies

Babies over one year will normally be eating family foods and these can be stored in the fridge for up to 48 hours. Always check 'use by' dates on commercial food and never give babies food which is out of date.

Foods which are more likely to cause food poisoning should not be given to babies and toddlers under about five years. These foods include:

- *shellfish which is raw or undercooked*
- *fish which is raw or undercooked*
- *meat which is raw or undercooked*
- *raw or undercooked eggs – cook them until the yolk is no longer runny*
- *unpasteurized milk, cheese and yogurt.*

Whole nuts may cause choking or will cause distress if a baby or toddler inhales one. They are not recommended for babies and toddlers under five years.

END-OF-CHAPTER QUESTIONS

1 *Until your baby is what age should you sterilize bottles and teats used for his milk-feeds?*

2 *Do you need to sterilize cups used for giving your baby drinks of milk and water?*

3 *Why should you add water above 70°C/158°F to powdered formula milks?*

4 *Where in the fridge should bottles of milk be stored if you store expressed breast milk or make up milk formula feeds in advance?*

5 *Which babies are at highest risk of illness from bacterial contamination of feed?*

6 *Why should you not use a microwave oven for heating bottles of milk for your baby?*

7 *How should you cool a feed before giving it to your baby?*

8 *How should you heat foods for babies?*

9 *Which foods should not be given to babies up to about five years of age as they are most likely to cause food poisoning?*

10 *How should you thaw frozen food and drinks for your baby?*

12

....

Looking ahead

In this chapter you will learn:
- *how to maintain a good relationship with food*
- *about setting boundaries to cope with your baby's preference for sweet food*
- *about preventing obesity*
- *about the importance of limiting convenience food and salt.*

If you have followed the advice in this book so far you should have a baby who looks forward to each meal as a positive and pleasant experience and enjoys eating a fairly wide range of foods.

Maintaining a good relationship with food

As your baby grows into a toddler, try to maintain your baby's positive approach to food:

▶ *Eat with your baby as often as possible.*
▶ *When you are eating with your baby eat the foods you want him to eat.*
▶ *Make positive comments about food.*
▶ *Talk about the foods you are eating – the colour, the taste, where it comes from.*

Remember that you are a strong role model for your baby and he will continue to learn by copying you as he grows up.

As he becomes more adept, involve him in your food shopping –
encourage him to help take things off the shelf and put them into
the supermarket trolley. Take him to well laid out market stalls or
greengrocers and allow him to choose a fruit or a vegetable – ask
the greengrocer to put his choice in a paper bag so that he can
carry it home.

Involve him in as much meal preparation as he can manage – ask
him to help set the table or count out foods to go into a bowl,
e.g. 'Put four bread rolls into a basket and put it on the table.'

Coping with preferences for sweet food

Babies, toddlers and older children naturally like sweet foods and
energy-dense foods which are high in fat and sugar, e.g. biscuits,
cakes, chocolate, ice cream, pastries and puddings. Toddlers will
over-eat these foods if given the opportunity so they need to be
limited but not completely denied. If you deny your child these
foods they will become more desirable as he sees other people
enjoying them. Include them in small quantities, from time to time,
especially as part of a celebratory meal. Enjoyment of food and
other activities is an important part of his emotional wellbeing.

He will crave sweet food and ask for it when he sees it. It is
important you set limits and stick to them – children feel secure
when they have limits and boundaries. Think about a reasonable
limit that suits you and your family and stick to it. If you keep
changing the boundaries and limits by saying no at first but then
giving in to a tantrum and saying yes, he will become confused
about where the boundary is. When he is upset and perhaps

throwing a tantrum in frustration at not having what he wants, he needs to learn that the stress of not having something will go away. Stick to your limits and negotiate a solution, e.g. 'You cannot have it now but we will have some for tea tonight.' Alternatively find a distraction, e.g. 'Let's look for a game and play it together.'

Limit sugary foods to a maximum of four times per day, e.g. all three meals and one snack.

Sugary foods include: sweetened breakfast cereals, puddings, cakes, biscuits, pastries, fruit purées, fruit juice, dried fruit, sweets, chocolate and sweetened drinks. Toddlers and children who do not have sugary foods more than four times per day are less likely to get tooth decay.

Don't use sweet food as rewards or bribes because it makes those foods seem more desirable than others which are not being used as rewards.

Better rewards are your time with him – promise to spend extra time with him playing or reading a book. If you encourage a toddler to eat vegetables so that he can have the pudding he will understand that pudding is a desirable food and the vegetables are so awful you need a reward to eat them.

Preventing obesity

With obesity rising in children it is important to get into the habit of encouraging toddlers to have opportunities for active play every day. They will be developing the co-ordination needed to enjoy sports and physical activity when they are older as well as burning up some energy.

Always allow babies and toddlers to eat to their appetite so that they know when they have had enough and are no longer hungry for more food. Never insist that they finish everything on their plate.

There is a feedback mechanism: when the stomach signals that it is full the brain signals a feeling of satiety and eating should stop. Obese children are unaware of when they have satisfied their hunger and are no longer hungry.

Keep foods to mealtimes and planned snacks and don't give high-fat foods such as packet snacks, like crisps, to keep your child occupied or quiet.

Convenience foods are usually higher in salt, fat and sugar and lower in fruit and vegetable content than home-cooked foods. They are now part of everyone's lives and if they are part of your family foods then you will want to use them for your children. Limit them and always serve small portions of them and add some extra fruit and vegetables. This can be simple raw fruits and vegetables which need minimal preparation. They will serve to lower the calorie content of the meal and add extra nutrients which are likely to be low in the convenience foods.

Salt

Do not encourage a liking for foods with added salt. Salty foods in small amounts will do no harm to children, but not encouraging a preference for salty foods may help prevent a rise in blood pressure with age. It is therefore better to flavour foods with herbs and spices rather than salt. Processed foods, which are high in sodium and salt, should also be avoided and salty snacks such as crisps should be given only occasionally.

END-OF-CHAPTER QUESTIONS

1 *Why should you eat with your baby as often as possible and eat the foods you want him to eat?*

2 *Which taste are babies born with a preference for?*

3 *How many times a day can a baby over 12 months have sweet food without increasing the risk of dental caries?*

4 *How do you successfully limit the amount of sweet food your baby eats?*

5 *Why is it wrong to give food as a reward, particularly sweet food?*

6 *Should you only give your baby a dessert if he finishes his savoury course?*

7 *Why is it wrong to insist that babies finish everything on their plate?*

8 *What are better rewards than food rewards?*

9 *Why should you keep your baby's salt intake low?*

10 *What can you use to flavour your baby's food in place of salt?*

Appendix 1

Nutrients and their food sources

During the first months of life babies get all their nutrients from their milk whether it is breast milk or one of the formula milks for babies.

By about six months of age, milk alone will not provide enough nutrients and energy or calories to keep babies growing normally. From this time on foods will play an increasingly important role in providing those nutrients.

Nutrient	Function in the body	Food sources
Protein	Provides structure for all the cells in the body. It is also part of enzymes and carrier molecules.	Milk will be the major source of protein throughout your baby's first year. After this, when milk is cut down, other foods will begin to provide more and more of the protein he needs. In his second year the main sources will be milk, yogurt, cheese, *(Contd)*

		meat, fish, eggs, nuts (chopped and ground or as butter) – see page 263 for caution with whole nuts*.

Other good sources of protein are pulses such as lentils, baked beans, humous and other starchy beans: chickpeas, butter beans and red kidney beans.

Cereals and foods containing flour such as bread, chapatti and pasta also provide small amounts of protein. |
| **Carbohydrate**
There are three types:

1. 'Simple' sugars, such as lactose in milk, fructose in fruit and added sugar – sucrose and glucose.
2. Starch.
3. Fibre which is made up of carbohydrate complexes which are unabsorbed. | Starch and sugar provide energy (calories). | Potatoes, yams, breakfast cereals, couscous, rice and any foods containing flour such as bread, chapatti, pasta, biscuits and cake.

Fruit contains the sugar fructose. |

		Milk contains the sugar lactose. Sweetened foods contain sugar and glucose.
Fibre Also called 'non-starch polysaccharides'. Fibre includes: ▶ non-digestible carbohydrates, mostly derived from plant materials, that are fermented in the colon ▶ prebiotics.	Fibre keeps the intestines functioning normally. Too little will cause constipation but too much can cause diarrhoea and could slow growth.	Babies do not need a lot of fibre but they will get some from fruits and vegetables, cereals and foods made from flours. White flour and breads contain some fibre while wholemeal and wholegrains contain more. Wholegrain cereals such as porridge, Ready Brek and Weetabix contain more fibre than most processed cereals.
	Prebiotics feed the bacteria in the colon which are important in the normal functioning of the intestines – mainly the colon.	Prebiotics are found in some fruits and vegetables.

(Contd)

Fat

It is made up of

1. Fatty acids which may be medium or long-chains which are:

▶ saturated
▶ monounsaturated
▶ polyunsaturated including omega 3 and omega 6.

2. Complex fats, e.g. cholesterol and phospholipids.

Provides energy and carries some vitamins around the body.

All cells have fats in their structure.

We can make all the fats we need except the omega 3 and omega 6 fats which we need to have in our food. They are needed for all cells in the body. Babies' cells in the brain, nerves and skin contain very high levels of omega 3 and omega 6 fats.

Oils and fats used in cooking foods.

Butter, margarine and other spreads for bread.

Cream and cheese.

Cakes, biscuits and ice cream.

Small amounts in whole milk, yogurt, egg yolks and lean meat.

Babies need a good balance of omega 3 and omega 6 fats. There are usually plenty of omega 6 fats in the diet.

Oily fish are good sources of omega 3 long-chain fats, DHA (docosahexaenoic acid) and EPA (eicosapentaenoic acid).

Rapeseed oil and walnut oil are good sources

		of omega 3 ALA (alpha-linolenic acid). Most pure vegetable oil in the UK is made from rapeseed oil. Olive and soya oils have a good balance of omega 3 and omega 6.
Water	For maintaining normal hydration, blood pressure and fluid balance. Babies' bodies are about 70 per cent water.	Drinks – milk, fruit juices and diluted squashes are all about 90 per cent water. Soups, sauces and fruit and vegetables have high water contents.
Vitamins Vitamin A (carotene)	Ensures normal growth and development, strengthens the immune system, important for healthy intestines, skin and good vision.	Whole cows' milk. Egg yolks. Butter and margarine. Orange, red and dark green fruit and vegetables such as carrots, red peppers, *(Contd)*

		tomatoes, sweet potato, pumpkin, apricots, mangoes, cantaloupe melons, broccoli.
		Oily fish.
		Liver and liver paté have very high levels so only give them to your baby once per week.
B vitamins Include thiamine, folic acid, niacin (nicotinamide), riboflavin, pyridoxine, biotin, pantothenic acid and vitamin B12.	Growth and development of healthy nervous system. Involved in the processes that convert food into energy for your baby.	Liver paté and yeast extracts such as Marmite are the only foods that contain all the B vitamins. Most breakfast cereals are fortified with extra B vitamins. Other good sources are meat, milk, yogurt, cheese, fish, eggs, seeds, bread and vegetables.
Vitamin C (ascorbic acid)	Helps absorb iron from non-meat sources.	Most fruit and vegetables contain some.

	Is part of the immune system and protects cells from damage. Maintains blood vessels, cartilage, muscle and bone.	The richest sources are blackcurrants, kiwi fruit, citrus fruits, tomatoes, peppers and strawberries. Potatoes, sweet potatoes and mangoes are also good sources. Certain fruit juices such as blackcurrant and orange have higher levels than other fruit juices.
Vitamin D	Needed to absorb calcium into the body, and to regulate calcium levels in the blood.	Most vitamin D is made in the skin when babies are outside during the summer months, i.e. April–September in the UK. It is the ultraviolet sunlight which acts on skin to make vitamin D. Oily fish contain vitamin D and babies enjoy fishcakes or fish pie made with oily fish. *(Contd)*

		Some yogurts, fromage frais and one or two breakfast cereals have vitamin D added to them.
		Follow-on milks and growing-up milks are enriched with it.
Vitamin E	Antioxidant that protects cell structures throughout the body.	In a wide variety of foods.
		Rich sources are vegetable oils, margarine, avocados, almonds, meat, fish and eggs.
Vitamin K	Blood clotting.	Mainly produced by bacteria in the large bowel.
		Rich food sources are green leafy vegetables and broccoli.
Minerals Calcium	Needed for growing bones and the new teeth forming in the gums.	Richest sources are milk, cheese, yogurt and fortified soya milk.

	It is also important in muscle contractions, responses to hormones, and for the structure of all cells and the working of nerves.	White bread is fortified with calcium. Ground almonds. Canned fish with bones such as sardines.
Copper	Making energy and protein.	In small amounts in most foods.
Fluoride	Strengthens tooth enamel and makes it resistant to attack by bacteria, which cause tooth decay.	A smear of fluoride toothpaste on the toothbrush when cleaning teeth twice a day provides enough. It is in tap water in areas of the UK where tap water is fluoridated or the water naturally contains adequate levels of fluoride. However, there are large areas of the UK where water does not contain adequate fluoride. In these areas dentists often recommend *(Contd)*

		fluoride drops for babies. Ask your dentist for advice as giving a baby too much fluoride can cause permanent brown spots on teeth.
Iodine	Part of the hormone thyroxine, which helps convert food into energy and is needed for mental and physical development.	Fish, milk, yogurt and eggs.
Iron	Necessary for carrying oxygen around the body in the blood and is needed for growing muscles, energy metabolism and the immune system.	Best sources are red meat (beef, lamb and pork) and dark poultry meat, e.g. chicken legs and thighs. White meat such as chicken breast has less. Other sources are: ▶ fortified breakfast cereals ▶ ground or chopped nuts (see page 263 for caution with whole nuts*)

		▶ dhal, lentils, humous ▶ poppadoms made with lentil flour ▶ bhajis made with chickpea flour. Smaller amounts are in fruit and vegetables.
Magnesium	Helps to convert food into energy and is needed for bone development and protein production.	Best sources are wholegrain breakfast cereals, milk and yogurt. Also in meat, egg, dhal, lentils, humous, potatoes and some vegetables.
Phosphorus	Needed for bone growth and energy metabolism.	Richest source is milk. Present in most other foods.
Potassium	Important for fluid balance, muscle contraction and for the nerves to function correctly.	Milk, vegetables and potatoes. Bananas, dried apricots, prunes, dates and kiwi fruit are also good sources. *(Contd)*

Selenium	Antioxidant.	Meat, fish, vegetables and cereals.
Sodium	Regulation of fluid balance and blood pressure.	Salt is the main source of sodium and salt is used in making bacon, ham, cheese and bread. Sodium is also found in meat, milk and yogurt. Salt added in cooking or to cooked foods is not needed for babies. Foods with added salt such as crisps and processed foods should be kept to a minimum.
Zinc	Involved in the function of many enzymes and hormones.	Best sources are meat, fish and shellfish and eggs. Other good sources are milk, wholegrain breakfast cereals

		such as porridge, Shredded Wheat, Weetabix, and bread.
		Some in potatoes, dhal, lentils, humous and leafy vegetables.
Phytonutrients Substances in plants, which provide long-term protection against cancer and heart disease. Also called flavanoids, flavanols, isoflavones. Examples: lycopene lutein and quercertin.	They act as antioxidants protecting all cells from damage and they are an important part of the immune system.	All fruit and vegetables, especially those that are brightly coloured. Cocoa and chocolate.

Whole nuts should not be given to children under five years old because of the risk of inhalation and choking.

Appendix 2

Recipe index

Answers to end-of-chapter questions

Chapter 3

1 Honey and foods with added salt or sugar.
2 From six months.
3 From about six months.
4 A cup of water, as your baby may be thirsty.
5 Meat, oily fish, fortified breakfast cereals, pulses, ground and crushed nuts and vegetables.
6 From about seven to eight months.
7 Keep giving this food, as he needs more practice at managing lumps.
8 It helps him develop a positive attitude to food and to learn self-feeding skills.
9 Turns his head away, keeps his mouth shut, may push the spoon or plate away.
10 One third meat, fish, eggs, pulses or nuts; one third starchy food such as potatoes, rice or pasta; one third vegetables.
11 You need to continue to sterilize milk bottles and teats until your baby is one year old, but cups are much easier to keep clean and do not need to be sterilized.
12 Breastfed babies should begin at six months, unless they have been advised to begin earlier. Formula-fed babies should begin when they cut down their intake of milk to less than 500 ml/17 fl oz per day.

Chapter 4

1 Anytime from about nine to ten months old, as it is better for your baby to begin eating more solid food at breakfast.

2 At around nine to ten months.
3 Raw foods such as raw carrot and cucumber sticks and raw apple slices.
4 From about 12 months, but change to cups anytime from around nine months.
5 The number of milk-feeds and the amount of milk drunk.
6 When he is drinking less that 500 ml/17 fl oz formula milk each day. Breastfed babies should have begun at around six months of age.
7 So that babies can watch others eating, because they learn by copying others.

Chapter 5

1 All babies born before 37 weeks' gestation.
2 13 weeks $(40 - 27 = 13)$.
3 For two years if he was born before 32 weeks' gestation and for one year if he was born after 32 weeks' gestation.
4 The risk of NEC is lower and the growth hormones in breast milk help development and growth.
5 Because they are not able to suckle well enough to take all their milk orally.
6 At about 35 weeks' gestation.
7 They have not accumulated the same body stores of certain vitamins and minerals as term babies.
8 Between five and eight months after their actual birth date.
9 Good head and neck support to prevent them choking.
10 More likely.

Chapter 6

1 2.4 kg/5 lb compared with 6.6 kg/14½ lb in their first year.
2 Because milk is very low in iron and babies over one year need to eat a lot of iron rich foods in place of milk.
3   1 *Bread, rice, potatoes, pasta and other starchy foods*
    2 *Fruit and vegetables*

    3 *Milk, cheese and yogurt*
    4 *Meat, fish, eggs, nuts and pulses*
4 Foods high in fat and/or sugar.
5 By giving him a variety of food from the four nutritious food groups.
6 Vitamins A and D.
7 Twice a day.
8 A smear of fluoridated toothpaste.
9 Babies like routine and do not eat well if they are tired or over-hungry.
10 It provides two opportunities to give your baby nutritious foods and it makes the meal more interesting for him.

Chapter 7

1 Iron, zinc, omega 3 fats and vitamin D.
2 Protein, iron, zinc, calcium and vitamins A, D, K, B2, B12.
3 Because it is unlikely to provide adequate nutrients for optimal growth and development.
4 A combination of nuts or pulses and starchy foods such as rice, pasta, potatoes and bread.
5 Vegetarian babies can be changed to cows' milk at 12 months, but it is preferable for them to remain on breast milk or a formula milk as these provide a wider range of nutrients than cows' milk.
6 Rapeseed and walnut oil and ground or chopped walnuts.

Chapter 8

1 It is a normal stage in their development when they become wary of eating new and unfamiliar foods.
2 Fear of the new.
3 Yes.
4 At around 18 months.
5 The vast majority of babies grow out of it, but a very small number do not.

6 Constipation, reflux, anaemia, high temperature, pain or discomfort.

7 He is: not hungry, tired, over-hungry, anxious, sad, lonely, insecure or his attention is distracted away from the meal.

8 He does not like the taste or the texture, or he is wary of the food because it is new to him or unfamiliar.

9 By overestimating how much their baby needs to eat, by coercing their baby to eat more when he does not want to, by giving their baby more attention when they do not eat than when they do.

10 Parents of babies who were born prematurely are often more anxious, as are parents of babies who became very ill early in life.

Chapter 9

1 They gain less weight in their second year – about 2.4 kg/5 lb – compared with a weight gain of about 6.6 kg/14½ lb in their first year.

2 Not common, only about 1 in 12 babies react to food.

3 Most babies grow out of their food allergy by the age of five years.

4 No, only those babies likely to have an anaphylactic reaction need to be prescribed an EpiPen.

5 Fruit juices, squashes and fizzy drinks.

6 Those with a poor diet and particularly those who drink too much milk.

7 Small frequent meals rather than large meals.

8 Formula-fed babies.

9 Babies with dark skin.

10 Vitamins A and D as babies are unlikely to get enough of these two vitamins from their food.

Chapter 10

1 No.

2 Added sugar, salt and pesticides.

3 Vitamin C and folic acid.
4 No.
5 Omega 3 fat.
6 Oily fish.
7 Rapeseed oil.
8 Lactose in milk, fructose in fruit and honey, maltose in starchy foods.
9 Iron and calcium.
10 Vitamins A and D.

Chapter 11

1 Until 12 months of age.
2 No, because it is easier to scrupulously clean cups than bottles and teats.
3 To kill any bacteria that may be in the powdered formula milk.
4 At the back of the fridge, not in the shelves on the door.
5 Preterm babies, young babies under about two months old and babies who are already ill.
6 Milk heats unevenly and can contain hot spots. In addition it carries on heating after it is taken out of the microwave.
7 Hold the capped bottle under running water, and test the temperature to make sure it is about the same as body temperature by dropping a little milk onto the inside of your wrist.
8 Heat them to piping hot right through to kill off any bacteria and then cool before feeding to your baby.
9 Raw or undercooked fish, shellfish, meat, eggs and unpateurised milk, cheese and yogurt.
10 In the fridge so that the temperature of the food or drink does not rise above 5°C/41°F.

Chapter 12

1 Babies learn by copying, and you are a strong role model for your baby.
2 A sweet taste.

3 Four times, for example, at three meals and for one snack.
4 Decide on a healthy amount, set the limits and stick to them even when your baby throws a tantrum.
5 You make the foods given as a reward seem more desirable to your baby than other foods.
6 No, a nutritious pudding should always be given whether the savoury course is eaten or not.
7 Babies should be encouraged to perceive when their appetite is satisfied.
8 Spending time playing or reading with your baby.
9 If your baby develops a preference for salty foods and continues to eat a lot of salt, he is more likely to develop high blood pressure.
10 Herbs and spices.

Taking it further

FURTHER READING

Bridget Wardley and Judy More (2004) *The Big Book of Recipes for Babies, Toddlers and Children*. Duncan Baird Publishers, London.

BREASTFEEDING SUPPORT GROUPS

Association of Breastfeeding Mothers, www.abm.me.uk
Helpline: 08444 122 949.

The Breastfeeding Network, www.breastfeeding.co.uk
Helpline: 0844 20 909 20.

La Leche League, www.lalecheleague.org.uk
Helpline: 0845 120 2918.

National Childbirth Trust, www.nct.org.uk
Helpline: 0300 330 0771.

FOOD SCARES

The Food Standards Agency, www.food.gov.uk

NUTRITION INFORMATION

The British Dietetic Association, www.bda.uk.com
Child-nutrition.co.uk, www.child-nutrition.co.uk
The Food Standards Agency, www.food.gov.uk
Infant and Toddler Forum, www.infantandtoddlerforum.org
Little People's Plates, www.littlepeoplesplates.co.uk
Nutrition Society, www.nutritionsociety.org

PRETERM BABIES

BLISS – the premature baby charity
68 South Lambeth Road, London, SW8 1RL
www.bliss.org.uk

TWINS AND TRIPLETS

Twins and Multiple Births Association TAMBA,
www.tamba.org.uk
www.twinsclub.co.uk

COPING WITH ALLERGIES

www.allergyaction.co.uk
www.allergyuk.org
www.anaphylaxis.org.uk
www.coeliac.org.uk

HALAL COMMERCIAL BABY FOODS

www.mumtaz.co.uk

ORGANIC FOODS AND FARMING METHODS

Soil Association, www.soilassociation.org

Sustain. The Alliance for better food and farming,
www.sustainweb.org

THE VEGETARIAN SOCIETY

Parkdale, Dunham Road, Altrincham, Cheshire, WA14 4QG.
Tel. 0161 925 2000.
www.vegsoc.org
www.vegsource.com for vegetarian recipes.

Glossary

allergen A substance that causes an immune response.

amino acids A group of compounds that make up proteins.

atopic Someone who has atopy.

atopy A genetic tendency to develop immediate allergic reactions to substances such as pollen, food and insect venoms. Manifested by hay fever, asthma, food allergies, eczema or similar allergic conditions.

dehydration The condition that results from excessive loss of body water – this may occur due to a high temperature and excessive sweating or it may be due to normal water losses through the skin, breathing, and passing water and stools coupled with an inadequate intake of water.

EDD Estimated Date of Delivery. For premature babies this is the date they were expected to be born if they had remained in the womb for a normal length pregnancy of 40 weeks' gestation.

gastro-oesophageal reflux See *reflux*.

gluten A protein found in wheat, rye and barley. Oats contain a very similar protein.

halal Means 'lawful' and relates to meat which is acceptable to Muslims. Meat needs to be ritually slaughtered to be halal.

kosher Means that animals and birds have been slaughtered by the Jewish method, carried out by a trained and authorized person.

oesophagus The part of the digestive canal that food and drinks pass through between the throat down to the stomach.

Personal Child Health Record (PCHR) In England this is a red book in which healthcare professionals record details about your baby's health, records of immunizations and any measurements of weight, length and head circumference.

pesticides Chemicals including herbicides, insecticides and fungicides used in farming to kill pests.

phytonutrients These are substances in plants, which boost the immune system and provide long-term protection against cancer and heart disease. They include the brightly coloured pigments in fruits and vegetables and are also called flavanoids, flavanols and isoflavones.

phyto-oestrogens Plant chemicals that behave the same way in the body as the hormone oestrogen.

preterm babies Babies born before 37 weeks' gestation.

protein A complex molecule consisting of a particular sequence of chains of amino acids. Proteins are essential constituents of all living things.

red book See PCHR.

reflux, or gastro-oesophageal reflux The contents of the stomach flow backwards, up and out of the stomach into the oesophagus.

stool Evacuated faecal matter passed through the anus. It is commonly called poo.

term babies Babies born after 37 weeks' gestation.

Index